From Eastman to Victoria

CLAUDETTE R. EWENS

From Eastman to Victoria
Copyright © 2024 by Claudette R. Ewens

All rights reserved. No part of this publication may be reproduced, distributed, or transmitted in any form or by any means, including photocopying, recording, or other electronic or mechanical methods, without the prior written permission of the author, except in the case of brief quotations embodied in critical reviews and certain other non-commercial uses permitted by copyright law.

Tellwell Talent
www.tellwell.ca

ISBN
978-1-77962-174-0 (Paperback)
978-1-77962-175-7 (eBook)

Prologue

I was born in 1940 in Magog, a small Quebec town, a bindle across my back. I finally laid my bindle down in beautiful Victoria in 2023.

Now, sitting comfortably in my apartment overlooking the Pacific, I believe it is high time that somewhere be recorded the adventures of my life before all these memories that flit like butterflies in my brain fly away into the cosmos …

My story is sometimes sad, sometimes funny but never dull. I hope you will enjoy reading it.

Acknowledgments

All my gratitude to you, my dear Ginette, for your patience and encouragement.

Many thanks to my friends Gaston Cantin, Yvon Belair, Chéryl Tremblay, Nadia Sheikh, Claude Bégin, and Richard Stimpson, for your support.

Thank you, my dear cousins Monic and Lynda Cunningham for your positive comments.

I

On September 17, 1916, you can hear the bells ringing from the small white church in honour of the baptism of Lea Laplante. Her parents Rose Bernais and Felix Laplante live nearby on a farm in the small Eastern Townships of Eastman, Quebec. They already have a daughter, Olida, and two sons, Oliva and Ovide. Although good Catholics, Rose and Felix have decided not to follow the dictate of the church which is to have twenty or so children for the so-called "revenge of the cradle." However, they later will have a last one more child, Leola. Lea is a handful, gifted with a keen intelligence, she will overcome many difficulties in her life but in so doing will become hard and merciless. Rose and Felix are not rich but still better off than their neighbours. Lea always has extra food in her lunch box which she shares with her less-fortunate classmates.

Thus, popular and mischievous, on this beautiful fall day Lea suggests to her classmates that they go picking wild strawberries in the field at lunchtime. They follow her but none return to class in the afternoon. Miss Lucier, their teacher is most upset and complains to Felix. Mr. Laplante is taken aback but he is an indulgent man, and he loves his daughter. Lea receives but a slight reprimand.

At fourteen, her brother Ovide is dying downstairs of tuberculosis. She is up in her room on her knees praying for him when suddenly he appears on the wall facing her, wearing a cassock. He always wanted to be a priest but Felix, their father, needed his son on the farm.

Lea is a good-looking young woman. On Saturday nights, it is party time at the Laplante's. She has plenty of suitors. She plays the piano by ear and sings. There are fiddlers and square dancing to liven up the evening. Poor Felix must retire at 8 p.m. because the cows must be milked at 4 a.m. the next day.

One beautiful Sunday afternoon Lea goes to the village a few kilometres away. She passes in front of the house where the Ewens live. A handsome young man tending the front garden spots her, likes what he sees, and throws a flower at her. Lea has just met her William.

Bill (the name he would go by for the rest of his life) was born on January 5, 1913, the second son of

Alice Mahony and William Riley Ewens. Alice is a sweet motherly woman. William Riley is a tall, dry, strict descendant of Scottish immigrants who arrived in the Eastern Townships of Quebec in the 18th century.

William is the Justice of the Peace in Eastman. He owns woodlots there and in Antigonish, Nova Scotia. He owns a sawmill where he cuts and stores wood. He is wealthy.

Young Bill, unlike his brother Neil, has no great ambition; he skips school and spends his days walking in his father's woods. In fact, the woods will remain his favourite place throughout his life. This handsome young man knows how to charm a lady! He courts Lea, she falls in love with him and eventually accepts his proposal of marriage. Their mixed marriage is audacious for the times. It is well accepted by the Laplante family, not so well accepted by the Ewens, and frowned upon by the Catholic Church who refuses to marry the couple in church.

Instead, they are married in the sacristy under the condition of raising their progeny as good Catholics. In 1939, the newlyweds move to Bowker Lake in a cottage owned by William Riley. It has a large veranda facing the lake, the perfect place for a honeymoon! On a beautiful April afternoon, on their way back from the general store, they decide to relax under a tree … one thing leads to another, and I am conceived.

To earn a living, the young couple runs a small restaurant. Lea prepares and serves meals, and Bill entertains the customers, often taking them fishing in his rowboat while Lea is sweating in the kitchen. Bill is having an enjoyable time. Adding to her burden, Lea often receives her sister Olida with her husband Conrad, she likes having them around on weekends, but it is more work for her.

I come to life on January 19, 1940, in my grandmother's bed in Magog, the Laplante's having sold their farm and moved to John Street, near Lake Memphremagog. I am baptized on the same day in St. Patrick Church. My name is Mary Rose Claudette. I disappoint my mother for the first time very early: I have a protruding right ear (which I will have corrected as an adult) and not a single hair on my head. A year later when it grows out, the curls are so tight my mother cannot run a comb through them.

Come winter, the young Ewens family leaves Bowker Lake to go live for a year in one of the lumber camps belonging to Bill's father. It is a harsh winter. My father earns his living cutting trees while my mother takes care of me. She tries to prevent me from catching a cold and makes leggings for me out of deer skin; they go up to my diaper. My father is a good hunter and there is no shortage of game in these woods. But in the end, life becomes too harsh. It is time to leave. We move into a two-story house on Pine Street in Eastman. My grandparents live nearby, and William Riley holds the mortgage. The house is painted a beautiful cream colour and has a wraparound veranda and tall columns with embellishments. There's a barn behind the house to store hay in the fall, a field next to the railroad track, a few strawberry bushes, and a flower bed by the road.

By the side of the track there is a solitary wagon occupied by squatters; they play a mournful tune on their bagpipes in the evenings. The sound is so touching I could cry. I love it when my dad comes home from camp on the weekends. On Saturday nights we often go the movies in a huge hall where bats fly around at times. They bring me along to see *King Kong*; it scares me to death! I move around a lot, and I am a disturbance. Lea asks my dad to go up and spank me on our return. Upstairs, he bids me to cry out while he beats the bed covers with his belt.

On Sundays we visit my grandparents. Bill's younger brother Neil and Vera (his older sister) are there. My grandparents' house is big and full of light. I play with Stephen, a cousin who is my age, three years old. He has a big red fire truck and another with a crank to unload gravel. He also has toy soldiers who can be cranked up to make them march. Vera and her husband take us for a ride in their 1938 Chevy; we ride in the rumble seat. It is so fun! My grandmother Alice makes good cookies in the shape of animals with a lot of little colourful seeds shining on top. I like her very much. My mother and Vera go upstairs to smoke in secret while Grandfather reads his newspaper.

Bill returns to his father's camp on Mondays, taking with him the casseroles and pies that Lea has prepared. She is slowly but surely getting fed up with her life and starts to grumble when Bill comes home on Friday nights. Bill runs to Mommy to complain about his wife's increasingly difficult character. His father says, as expected, "I told you so." Lea gives birth to Carole, but she dies of pneumonia at two months old in the arms of Grandma Ewens. The little one is displayed on a white table in the large living room. She is in a minuscule coffin with a candelabra on each side. At the age of three, they tell me that she is gone forever. Bill blames Lea and things really start to deteriorate between them.

Lea hears rumours: there are call girls at the camp to amuse the lumberjacks during the week. Lea confronts her husband, she threatens him with a poker, and he skedaddles away. From quarrels to reconciliations, Bill finally leaves but not without having conceived a third child. Lea has a miscarriage at the Providence, the hospital in Magog while my grandparents Ewens look after me. I am wearing a little navy-blue dress with red buttons and a red collar. It makes me feel good.

When my mother comes home, she is sick. We are alone. She lies in bed day and night while I try to find something to eat in the cupboards. I find some soda crackers; they are still good even if mice have gnawed on the corners. After a few days I go out. Near the fence, I see a lady coming by, and I tell her that my mother is extremely sick and that we have nothing to eat. Mrs. Yvonne Stebenne, the wife of the gentleman who runs the post office, does not hesitate. She goes inside, notices our painful situation, and takes charge of us. She and Lea become particularly good friends. We often go to their apartment over the post office. They have a daughter my age. We play together, and Stella is in my class in school. She has beautiful long brown braids. I envy her; my mother keeps me in Shirley Temple curls, and she breaks two hairbrushes on my head doing so. I honestly believe she hates me. I look like Bill: same forehead, same nose, same lips.

In winter 1944 there is no more firewood in the shed. Lea shuts off most of the house. In the kitchen we now have a bed which we share, a table and chairs and a rocking chair by the window. Lea spends her evenings by the window smoking, reading cards and listening to her small radio. The milkman, a good neighbour, brings us a pint of milk every evening. He takes pity on us. My mother receives a six-dollar cheque monthly from a government program for mothers in need, that's her only income. She sells some pieces of clothing, and my red tricycle for a few dollars. Bill wants a divorce, my mother a separation with alimony. He gets help from his dad who hires a handsome officer to seduce her so that she can be accused of adultery.

This good-looking man in uniform knocks on our door, introduces himself and tells my mother that there is no vacancy at the hotel. It was suggested to him that he should try our house; there might be a room she could rent him for one night. Of course not, my mother is no fool! However, he can sit in the rocking chair downstairs for as long as he wants to. He sees the sad condition we are living in. The following day, he is back with a bag of groceries. We have lunch together, there are stuffed olives which I see for the first time. He returns and invites us to go with him to Granby where he has business to attend to. We spend the night at a hotel. I am left alone while they have a drink at the bar. I cry a lot; I too want to spend time with this handsome man! I want a new daddy. Of these few fine days remain only two photos. My mother is summoned to appear in court for my father's divorce hearing. This fine gentleman hired by my grandfather to seduce my mother, swears that she is an honest woman and that nothing compromising has happened.

Every Friday night we take the bus to my grandparent's house in Magog for the weekend. The bus driver pretends to punch the bus tickets, leaving us as close as possible to the house. The bus terminal is too far for my little legs.

My cousin Monic, Aunt Olida's daughter, is nine years old and lives with Grandma Rose. I am always so happy to see her, but my high-pitched voice annoys her, and she won't let me play with her beautiful set of dishes. Her father died when she was less than a month old, so her mom leaves Monic with Gramma Laplante while she works.

One Sunday night, back home in Eastman, someone hiding in the dark throws a stone at the lightbulb that my mother leaves lit when she is gone: another intimidating tactic to make us move. Lea puts her padlock on the door, and we leave by train for Montreal to spend some time at Aunt Olida's. We get off at Windsor Station where I see a man of colour for the first time. I am so fascinated that I don't notice the column in front of me and bump into it! My Aunt Olida runs a snack bar with her husband Conrad on the Plateau Montreal. They offer us a room in the back, and my mother helps her sister at the restaurant in return. I never ate so much ice cream and liquorice pipes in my life!

In 1945, the soldiers return glorious and parade on Saint-Hubert Street behind their tanks. They are proud they've defeated the Germans. Everyone has a small flag to wave to greet them. Come September, I'm five-years-old: time to start school. Lea gets me ready for the first day, making me repeat, "I'm five years old." When I arrive at school and I'm asked my name, I answer "Five years old." I love learning my ABCs and forming these letters on the pages of my brand-new notebook. It's like drawing.

The school is one kilometre away. I must walk along Route 112; it's dangerous, and I must look on both sides of the road before crossing. There are no school buses in this small town. Our school is a two-story country school. In the winter we keep our snowsuits on because the only heating source is a cast-iron stove in the center of the floor. When it is too cold to go home for lunch, we toast our bread on top of it. The toilets are at the back of the building; a wooden wall separates the girls from the boys.

There are holes in it. We plug them with a finger. The first floor is for Grade 1 to Grade 5 students, the second for Grade 5 to Grade 9 students. We in the lower grades quickly learn to write, count and much more by listening to the lessons given to the older students. My girlfriend Stella is sitting in front of the class bully who dips the tips of her brown braids into his inkwell. It's not easy for girls to share a class with boys! At recess I am always the last chosen at baseball. I am bad at sports. The other girls are not allowed to play with me because my parents are separated. Such are the prejudices of the time.

At home, it is always cold; we often run out of wood to keep the kitchen stove going. The Stebennes bring us wood from time to time. Mom wraps a hot iron in a towel and puts it in at the foot of the bed so that so we can fall asleep. At times the pipes freeze and there is a lot of damage. The plumber comes and doesn't charge my mother much. We are one family of many paupers in the village. Grandpa Ewens seems to have forgotten he has a granddaughter, he who has wood to waste at his sawmill.

We get some relief when we go to Magog—and this would be a great moment for me if my mother wouldn't make me practice the piano while I'm there instead of letting me play with my cousins. I must also go to Cecile's for piano lessons. I must cross a field to get to her house;

there's a small barking dog on the way that frightens me so. Cecile realizes that I do not have a great aptitude for piano: I do not see with my right eye, and it is difficult for me to read both music spans at once. After fifteen minutes or so she allows me to read the comics in *La Tribune* and gives me a treat to enjoy. Her and her husband Louis do not have children, so they spoil me. Back in Eastman, I get spanked for not practicing but I am stubborn, and I still avoid the piano as much as I can!

Leola and Gaston have a convenience store on Ste. Catherine Street in Magog. They ask my mother if she would care to run it for them for a while. We live in a room at the back. It is a hovel no less. We can hear mice running between the walls at night. I go to St-Patrick's School; I am in the second grade. It is quite a long walk to school, and Mom slips a chocolate bar in my pocket for comfort. A nice lady comes to the store often—her name is Edwilda Gaulin—my mom and her become quite friendly. Dada, as we call her, invites us to her chalet at the Brampton Lake Marsh. She and her husband Joe are very generous folks; they take us there almost every weekend. The chalet is very modest. Electricity does not run that way yet, so lanterns light up the place. Fortunately, there is water in the well and a bathroom inside. The Gaulins will be very present in our lives for a while.

Lea is fed up with the convenience store and rightly so. We go to my grandparents in Magog to finish the winter. Aunt Leola upstairs sees it as abuse and a great argument takes place between both sisters. My mother, ever the drama queen, decides to leave. It is a winter evening; I am wearing my pretty dark-green coat with it is almost-fur collar. We leave on foot for the long walk to the Gaulin's chalet. After a few kilometres, I cannot walk anymore. My mother knocks at a stranger's house and asks for shelter for the night. The next morning, we continue to the Gaulin's chalet where we stay for a few days before returning to Eastman. It is so cold that Mom demolishes the unused chicken coop to make firewood—she is doing her best.

Upon the arrival of summer, my sweet cousin Monic comes spend some time with us during the school holidays. I am so happy when she is around as my mother's mood improves considerably. In the afternoon we go picnicking and swimming at Silver Lake, not at the main beach but closer to home where wild blue irises grow and there is still debris from a train derailment that occurred in 1940.

I am now nine years old, in the fourth grade and the first of my class. One day I come home from school; as usual my mom is still at the Stebennes'. My key does not fit in the padlock (the bailiff had it changed when he went in and threw our modest belongings on the street). I sit down, mortified and humiliated as my classmates look at me from afar, pitying me. Even the bully Claude has a tear in his eye. My mother arrives shortly after, accompanied by the Gaulin's.

They own a pickup truck. While we sit quietly waiting, they go back to the Brampton Marsh to fetch it. We wait for few hours like sitting ducks for their return. By midnight, the truck is loaded up and our furniture is moved to a barn at the back of the Laplante's house. Later, everything will be sold at an auction for twenty-eight dollars, including my little stuffed squirrel that I loved so much.

The Gaulins take us in while Lea looks for a job. I travel with Joe every day to school in Magog. Mom soon gets a job at a South Stukeley hotel. She works in the grill as a server where she earns a small salary, plus room and board, and tips. The hotelier is affable; he bids me sing in the grill every Wednesday afternoon. The customers must pay me five cents for every song they ask me to sing; I know practically all the songs in the jukebox. Mother keeps my earnings in a matchbox. I love not having to go to school on Wednesdays! It is a small English school. I understand and speak English but writing it is a struggle for me. At this point, I am in the fifth grade. The boys are disgusting! They expose themselves to the girls from behind their desks and chase them during recess outside. I do not mention anything to anyone. I am afraid of being punished for having looked at things I should not have seen.

Meanwhile in Magog, my grandparents divide in two parts the first floor of their house. The smaller apartment is for us to rent at nineteen dollars per month. It has a long room for the kitchen and living room and a small bedroom where we share a sofa bed and the darn piano. We can cross to my grandmother's apartment through the cellar. Monic is no longer living with Rose and Felix. She has gone to live with her parents and a stepbrother, a little boy adopted from an orphanage. His name is Denis. I am so glad to leave South Stukeley.

My mother now has money saved and a new job as a salesperson at a clothing store on Main Street where she earns fifty cents an hour. Mr. Bond appreciates her work and invites us for dinner with his family. The Polish cook serves us cabbage rolls stuffed with rice and sesame seeds. We eat wholeheartedly. Their son JoJo is my age, ten years old. We play together in his room; he has his own record player. My mother will tell me later, "we don't play with Jews." She will all her life, be full of prejudices.

Lea has good taste. She covers the many windows with three-coloured Venetian blinds and buys a turquoise kitchen set with thickly upholstered chairs and chrome legs, as well as a comfortable Art Deco armchair that she places near the window next to her new 45-rpm record player. We spend so many great Sunday afternoons listening to country and western music records—bought in Newport, an American town near the border—with Grandfather Felix and his brother John who lives across the street. They talk, laugh, smoke and drink a few beers—life is good. Lake Memphremagog is just down the street. During summer we go swimming every weekend even after supper sometimes. We go less and less to the Gaulins.

Back at St. Patrick's Convent, I am in fifth grade, but I am out of the loop. I rank twenty-seventh out of twenty-eight students. The teacher, Miss Senecal recognizes my insecurities and helps me overcome my lack of self-esteem by having me start the Friday afternoon songs. She also fusses over my drawings. Bad at sports as always, during recess I continue taking piano lessons with Sister St. Gerard who teaches all the musical instruments and conducts the parish orchestra. She also leads the church choir of which I am a member. It is so much nicer to be singing hymns than listening to the boring priest preach his sermon and say mass in Latin, a language that no one understands. I also take up clarinet lessons—I want to be part of Sister St. Gerard's orchestra so badly.

School is out; it's summer again. Apart from my grandmother's old grey cat, with whom I share all my thoughts, I have only one friend who lives next door. Her name is Claudette like me. She comes to my house almost every day; I am forbidden to go to hers or anywhere else. I have fun with my cousins Manon and Lise who still live upstairs. We play acting, dressing up in long sequinned ball gowns. These dresses come out of a box that Great Aunt Coranna brought over when she came from the States to visit her elder sister Rose. We pretend to be rich Americans, noses up in the air while speaking broken French. So, summer passes pleasantly enough between swimming, my cousins upstairs, and my friend next door.

Now let me tell you about Coranna. The youngest of thirteen children living on the Laplante's farm, she left at a young age for the United States of America to find work. A Connecticut copper company hires her in their factory. The young son who supervises the family plant finds her beautiful and falls in love with her. He courts her and sends her to finishing school. He then introduces her to his parents and is allowed to marry her. This beautiful young girl fresh from the farm in Eastman turns into a rich and elegant lady who dines in long dresses and meets her wealthy friends for their 4 p.m. tea.

When I am twelve years old, my mother admonishes me to stay away from boys. In our parish Father Dionne looks after us young people; he is loved by us all. He is a member of Sister St. Gerard's orchestra. He often helps us clean our musical instruments. He notices that I am having a hard time at home, especially after seeing me with a bad wound—this had resulted from a hit on the back of the head where my mother struck me with the heel of her high-heel shoe. She is getting meaner with me all the time because of her paranoia about boys, I guess. I often go to the presbytery on Sundays to have a chat with Father Dionne; he listens, he understands, and never preaches. But tongues start wagging. I am daydreaming in class while Sister Alexina is teaching a lesson. She calls out to me in front of the whole class, "Claudette, you should listen to the lesson rather than be dreaming of the vicar!" I run out of the classroom and dash across the street to the presbytery. I tell Father Dionne what happened. There is a big to-do afterwards; everyone in class is interviewed. All I know is that from then on Sister Alexina is very correct with me.

Summer comes around again. My cousin Monic visits us in Magog, and we meet her beau, Andrew

Cunningham. What a handsome fellow! He has black hair with curls low on his forehead and wears a zoot suit, the pants falling in folds over his shoes—it's the latest 1950s Chicago fashion. He is truly sympathetic; we all like him instantly. Another surprising event this summer: my father who now lives in Toronto with Sarah, visits his parents in Eastman for a couple of weeks. He spends a lot of time with my mother. It does look a lot like a second honeymoon. Dad even buys me a red bicycle.

In 1953 Monic and Andrew get married. Olida, her mother, hosts a small reception at her apartment. I sing an appropriate song and after a toast to the newlyweds we partake in my aunt's good buffet. They are the perfect couple. I like Larry, Andrew's younger brother; we even share a brief kiss in a quiet corner. A year later at the age of eighteen, Monic, with great difficulty, gives birth to Lynda. She will be throughout her life, the pride and joy of her parents.

Finally, in September 1954, I get a break from my mother—I attend teacher's college in Sherbrooke. It is a boarding school, and I go back home only for Christmas and the summer holidays. I don't have to share a bed with anyone, and the nuns are kind to me even if I don't have an ounce of piety in me! I have a crush on a classmate, and I express my emotions by writing a book full of poems that rhyme to perfection. Apart from algebra, geometry, and Latin and Greek history, we are taught good manners, correct French, and how to appreciate fine music. They have us listen to Ludwig van Beethoven, Franz Liszt, Bach and Schubert. It enthralls me.

Back home for the summer, I find our small apartment appalling. The low ceilings crush me, and I immensely hate having to share the sofa bed with my mother again. However, there is something new and exciting at my grandmother's apartment: they bought a television together. We watch it every night, some programs in English, others in French. It is still a rarity to own a television. There are folks who even watch it through store windows while sitting on the sidewalk. My grandfather, who died before ever seeing one, used to say that the reception would never get to Magog because of the mountains.

I go back to the college gladly for a second year. When the school year is over, I am told not to come back. With my lack of faith, I could not lead the young pupils towards the right path. So, I tell mother that I am no longer interested in teaching, and at sixteen years old, I feel ready to go to work. She was just waiting for that moment to move to Montreal.

My mother buys a rooming house on St. Andre Street, near Laurier. She has managed to save $5,000 for the deposit. We occupy a room that I must share with her, plus the kitchen. I would like to have my own room, there are few unoccupied. I mention it to her and there goes the drama queen again! She lays newspaper sheets on the kitchen floor, brings her blanket and pillow, and lays down ... then, says to me: "You want the room, take it."

We share the bathroom with the occupants of three bedrooms on the main floor. There is a lounge with a sofa and armchair and my piano. One of the boarders, Mrs. Garcia is a lovely French- and Spanish-speaking Algerian. She becomes my confidante. At one time, she dares to speak up for me while my mother is having supper; Lea throws her plateful at her.

I am hired by the phone company on Beaver Hill downtown. Having learned neither steno nor typing I must start at the bottom of the ladder. I sort, stamp, and distribute the mail throughout the office. Luckily for me, I am bilingual. I earn thirty-five dollars a week; my mother keeps thirty for room and board. I find a second job at a clothing store on Mount-Royal Street. I work there as a salesperson on Friday evenings. I find the assistant manager quite exciting. I also have chills for Kenny Titus, a James Dean-type of boy. We usually meet at noon at

Central Station. One day—a Friday, payday—Kenny and I take the train together for St. Eustache. It is my first fugue. We book a room for the night, but Kenny stays downstairs at the bar drinking my money away. I wait for him, but he never comes upstairs; he has gone back to Montreal. I feel very foolish.

Back in Montreal, I am too scared to go home. I knock at the presbytery of Christ Church on Ste. Catherine Street and tell my story to the Pastor. He calls my house, where Andrew and Monic are, my mother having called them in her distress. Andrew comes to pick me up; he is genuinely nice and reassuring to me. When I get home it is not a relieved mother of a prodigal daughter that receives me but a medieval matron who sends for a doctor to have my virginity checked out. Monic is in the room; the doctor is not allowed to see me alone. How humiliating. The young doctor just checks to be sure that I am not hurt in any way and asks me what I want him to say to my mother. The authorities, having been informed of my disappearance, they now consider me a delinquent. I must report regularly to a social worker of the Juvenile Court. I have also lost my job at the phone company, but I find another one quickly with a very well-known insurance company, thanks to my bilingualism. The breach between Lea and me is getting even wider.

At seventeen, I sing as an amateur in several low-end bars in the city. Another of Lea's great ideas. I always have stage fright and hate every moment of it. She has bought me a few strapless dresses in a fire sale. After a few days on the clothesline, they are quite fine. Of course, she always accompanies me. The social worker comes to check on how things are at home. She inspects my wardrobe. My mother shows her my fancy dresses, but the social worker is no fool; she can see that I do not have much of anything suitable to wear. At the expense of the Juvenile Court, she buys me a black and white skirt with a blouse to match. She knows that I am very unhappy and offers to send me to summer camp, but my mother is outright against it.

I have a weekend gig at a hotel; it is mid-December 1957. Coming through the lobby, I notice sitting in a corner the most handsome guy I have ever seen. Lea is not around, and I boldly walk up to him and kiss him on the mouth. I am totally infatuated! I return to the same hotel the following weekend to sing again. My handsome Italian is still there. He lives at the hotel. Away from my mother's gaze we get to know each other.

Back in Montreal, I make my second escape. Lea is in the kitchen; I'm in the living room. I play a few notes on the piano and put on a first boot, play a few more notes, and put on the other. A few more notes, and I take my coat out of the entrance closet and leave that house forever. I take the bus to join my handsome Michel. We spend a very beautiful Christmas together. He's worried: he's twenty-two and I am eighteen years old, he begs me to return to Montreal. I take refuge at Olida's where I spend New Year's. My aunt rents the upstairs to some Hungarian refugees, they come down and put garlands of flowers around my neck. It's so nice, I feel like a princess. I share a sofa –bed with Denis, my little cousin. Soon however, reality sets in. I must go meet my social worker. I am prevented from returning to my mother's, on account of the state of drunkenness she was in when reporting my absence. Hallelujah!

I now occupy a small room at a women's-only center in Cotes-des-Neiges, where I must be back before 1:30 a.m. I cheat of course. I go back to Rawdon every weekend. I buy a Berlitz Italian study book. I want to please Michel so much! Unfortunately, I am still a minor. I go to Juvenile Court for my monthly appointment with the social worker and they detain me. They have me disrobe and get in a bath that smells of disinfectant. I must undergo a gynaecological exam. I can't see the white coat and the navy-blue jumper I wore when I came in. They hand me a grey wraparound dress and escort me to a large room where there are several other young girls. They seem a lot cheekier than I am.

I must wait there until I get called to see the judge. Every time the door opens, I think it's my turn. It will take three weeks. I follow the routine, eat my baked beans and pieces of sausage. For dessert we have a slice of bread on which we spread molasses with the backs of our spoons as we are not allowed knives. After supper we return to the large room; I climb on the table and get the girls to sing along with me before retiring to the dormitory for the night. Mrs. Garcia comes to visit. She brings a toothbrush and some treats; she is the only one who bothers to come see me. Finally, the door opens, and this time it's my turn. I think I'm getting out, but not so fast! The judge sends me to a convent of the Sisters of the Good Shepherd on Sherbrooke Street for an indefinite time. It's for my protection, he says. When I get there, I'm given a yellow blouse and a navy-blue skirt to wear; it's the uniform. I am assigned a bed in the dormitory. They are many young delinquent girls held there like I am.

We spend mornings working. My first task is to wrap crêpe paper around wire stems to be set later under artificial flowers. In the afternoon we can study what we choose, if it is available. I learn how to type, and I keep at my Italian lessons. The nuns are kind to us, and we eat well. I get lucky: after a while I get to work in the kitchen with the Sisters. We make soup in a huge cauldron and prepare desserts sweetened with brown sugar. There's a barrel full, I dip my hand in as I pass by. The bread hutch is filled daily, and it smells good. After a while I am assigned another occupation in the sister's sewing room. I learn to mend their white habits. It is so calm and quiet in that room and there's a great view over St. Dominique Street where one can watch people go by. As a rule, we are not allowed near the windows but on this day of the St. John the Baptist Parade we are permitted to watch it go by. I see my Aunt Olida, Monic, Denis, and my mother on the sidewalk below. Not a look from mother towards me but Denis looks up with tears in his eyes. He knows how to charm the nuns who allow him to come see me on Sundays. He brings his hula hoop, puts on his little show, and they find him very cute and funny.

I attend mass every morning in the little chapel, just to show what a good girl I have become. This morning, I refuse to go to work; instead, I sit and listen to a nun playing Rachmaninoff wonderfully on the piano that is in the hall. I have been punished enough. Mother Superior summons me to her office. She says that they did all they could for me, and I could back to my job, with some restrictions. Miraculously, I get my old job back at the Insurance Company. I am to stay at the convent but at the front where the offices and an apartment with a few rooms are. Mother Genevieve gives me a nice room next to hers. It costs me ten dollars per week. There is a fridge full of good things in the kitchen. My trunk is brought in with my few possessions from my mother's house. The only caveat is that I must be in by 11 p.m. It is simply heavenly!

In August 1958, at lunchtime, I am walking on Dorchester Street. I see three young black men on the other side; the middle one has his arms around the shoulders of his friends. He spots me and crosses the street towards me. "I'm Paul Shepherd," he says. He has a great smile and wears his hair like Little Richard—well, almost. We chat for a while, and he wants to see me again. He lends me his bracelet and tells me to return it to him after work at the same place. I am fascinated; I keep the appointment and return his bracelet. He wears a ring with the caduceus symbol and tells me he is a medical student at McGill University. He is a darn good liar, and I believe everything he says. Thereafter, I see him every day. He is always there for me; I come to trust and rely on him. I feel loved and desired for the first time.

Mother Genevieve calls me to her office. Someone has told her that I was seen with a young man and why has she not been introduced to him yet? I hesitate, and she adds, "Is it because he is a man of colour?" "I did not think I had to," I replied, "but it will be my pleasure to do so." The meeting goes very smoothly, and I am allowed to keep going out with him. Mother Genevieve also tells me that an anonymous lady had called her about the same thing, and she had answered: "Mrs. Ewens, leave your daughter alone."

I try to reconcile with my mother. I knock at her door but as soon as she sees me, she casts a spell on me. She says, "I wish that your body rots and that your children will be monsters," and she shuts the door in my face. Nevertheless, I am happy. I spend my weekends with Paul; we often go the movies. He takes me to his aunt's apartment on St. Urbain Street and makes me great French fries. The place is pitiful, but the fries are great. One such afternoon, two tall and corpulent ladies barge in the apartment without knocking and start yelling at Paul: "What's going on here," they say. I find out that Paul lives here with his Japanese mistress Lili. That his name is Stanley Earl Shepherd, that he was born in Truro, Nova Scotia, and that these ladies have raised him since his mother died when he was four years old. All the lies were to impress me … and I love him still. Rich or poor, he will always be Paul to me! From then onwards we meet elsewhere; there are plenty of rooms for rent by the hour in the area.

Paul hates to be reminded of his childhood in Africville in Truro, where black folks had to sit upstairs at the movie theatre. They weren't allowed downstairs; it was for whites only. His ancestors were slaves brought to the West Indies, linked one to the other by a chain attached to an iron collar. He keeps a page from a *National Geographic* depicting this atrocity. The image haunts him still.

Months go by, and the holiday season is upon us. We are out with my little cousin Denis. He wants us to go to his mom's, my Aunt Olida. She refuses to receive us now that I am "living in sin," she says. I think it is more because she is terrified of Lea. On Christmas Eve, Mother Genevieve serves us a Christmas dinner. She doesn't sit with us; she is very discreet. What a wonderful person she is. On New Year's Eve, Paul and I arrive after curfew. She answers the door and says, "It's past 11 p.m., you will have to come back tomorrow." We spend our first night together.

On January 19, 1959, I am nineteen years old. I'm to return to the women's center on the following Friday. A plan is forming in my head which I share with Paul. He agrees with me: we will go live in Toronto. I call Monic before I go, but they are too busy to receive me. She doesn't know that I am leaving; she would warn my mother. I call Mrs. Garcia, tell her I am going to Toronto, and I would like to come and say goodbye. Once at her house, she gives me ten dollars to help.

Friday comes, my trunk is loaded in the taxi, and I tell the driver to take me to Central Station. Paul is waiting for me. We buy two tickets for Toronto. Paul tells me that he is not coming with me but that he will follow me later. He wants to be seen around after my disappearance so that he doesn't get accused of kidnapping a minor. He is twenty-three-years old, and I am still considered a minor at nineteen. I leave alone, with fifty dollars in my pocket, and two apples that taste of insecticide. I hope Mother Genevieve will forgive me.

I arrive at the Toronto train station early in the morning. I call my dad and ask him if he could come and get me. "Stay put," he says, probably reluctantly. He finds me too skinny, and he tells me I look like a DP (the acronym for a deported person). I spend a short time at his apartment. I have a few slices of bread that Sarah makes herself and ask my dad to help me find a furnished room. I find one on Crawford Street; it is on an upstairs flat. The bed looks comfortable, there's a fridge and a two-burner stove. I must share the bathroom. It costs only eleven dollars per week. Dad brings up my trunk and leaves.

Next, I go out for a few groceries and settle down. The next day I go job hunting and I am hired by coin dealers. I keep the inventory. Both partners steal from one and another. They remove coins and tell me not to record it.

I type a letter to Paul giving him my address. A few days later he knocks on my landlords' door and asks permission to go upstairs to join his wife. No problem, we will be lodging there for quite a while. There is hardly anything in his suitcase: his birth certificate, a few pieces of clothing, some records of Frank Sinatra, Ella Fitzgerald, Nat King Cole, and the infamous illustration of the chained slaves.

It is difficult for Paul to find work. He ends up working in a car wash. The days spent in the pit discourage him, and he returns to Montreal to his Japanese girlfriend. I am so sad. He comes back a week later. I guess he finally made his choice between me and Lili. This time, he finds a good job as a salesclerk in a hardware store.

We leave Crawford Street to move to a larger apartment. The owners are immigrants from Eastern Europe. Mrs. Goc is Ukrainian; at one time she had been held in a Siberian prison, and she had known great hardship before marrying Michael Goc, who is Polish. They are affable and generous people. We cannot go down to pay the rent without accepting a small glass of peach schnapps and a few blinis to go! I now work at a jewelry factory; I spend the day typing invoices. I buy a sewing machine and patterns. I have a new dress almost every week. Paul is easy to live with; he does more than his share. He cooks, does the shopping, and goes out to the laundromat. I am left with the dishes and the house cleaning. We are not rich, but we are comfortable.

We make good friends; Johnny and Isolene Giscombe are people Paul knows from Truro, and they live not too far from us. They invite us for supper; Isolene makes crisp pig-tail bites as starters and barbeque ribs to die for. Johnny has a great jazz record collection which we listen to in his basement. There's also an old classmate, Ben, who is married to a white girl. They have two boys and a little blond girl with tight ringlets. There is also Terry, a friend I made at work. We go fishing with her and her husband some weekends. Saturday nights we go to the cinema for the midnight shows; sometimes we watch three movies in a row and get out at daybreak! On Sundays, weather permitting, we take the ferry to the islands of Lake Ontario. It is mostly deserted. We bring a picnic box, our yellow transistor radio, and swim a little. These simple pleasures make me happy.

Finally, I am twenty-one-years old. I write to my cousin Monic and give her our address. She writes back that they will come down soon to see us. We need to get married right away, before they get here. I want her to report to Lea that her daughter is not living in sin. I sew a beautiful pale-blue suit for the occasion. We ask Aniela and Michael Goc to be our witnesses. They thought we were already married, but they accept willingly and without the slightest batting of an eye.

We find a nice protestant Pastor willing to marry us, a bi-racial couple, in his office where he has brought some bouquets of flowers from the church where he will celebrate another marriage later in the afternoon. Michael signs the register and guides Aniela's hand for her signature because she doesn't know how to write.

I am so happy to see Monic and Andrew after two years. They come by train to visit us in our humble apartment. We do not have much, our furniture is modest, and I decorate with covers from our vinyl records. Nevertheless, Monic and I have a lot of catching up to do while Andrew and Paul go play pool. When they leave, we promise to go and visit them in turn. I feel a bit nostalgic, but I am so happy to have seen them again. I think how much I would like to see Aunt Olida and Denis again. Perhaps I could even attempt a reconciliation with my mother.

In the meantime, I'm fed up with typing invoices all day and start searching for a more lucrative and rewarding position. I find a job in the accounting department of an advertising company in Don Mills, a suburb of Toronto. I take care of the accounts receivable; it is very easy to learn, and I like the creative environment.

We move to Scarborough near Don Mills in a newly built building. We rent a one-bedroom apartment. Quite an improvement, it even has a swimming pool in the back. We buy new furniture: a blue sectional sofa with a rotating bar in the middle. I make drapes to match, and Paul gets a recliner to watch comfortably all his sports on TV. In addition, we now have a credenza with a turntable built in to listen to our many stereo records. The bathroom is dusty pink—a brand-new colour—and the bedroom has a large wardrobe with folding doors. Everything is so modern! Paul gets a job in an office in Scarborough, and he buys his first car, a cream-coloured Sedan with power brakes and power steering. It also has a sloping electric back window that freezes and gets stuck in winter. He drives fast and nervously; I am so scared I often sit in the back.

Monic and Andrew invite us to come and celebrate Christmas Eve 1962 with them. More and more skilled on my sewing machine, I make a black velvet dress to wear for the occasion. It is a great party. I see all my beautiful people there except—you guessed it—my mother, who doesn't show up. She will complain later about having spent Christmas alone. It saddens me but not to the point of ruining this beautiful event. Paul is not fluent in French, but he understands it. We dance in the large living room; the ladies are very chic. Monic also sews her own clothes. She made herself a beautiful dress from a pattern: It has plunging V-shaped back, and she wears a string of beads that hangs in the back. The same thing goes for Jeanne, Andrew's sister. Montreal women are quite elegant and feminine. I chat with my cousin Denis: he is fifteen years old, has a few girlfriends, but admits that he is attracted to boys. I'm not the only one to have suspected it; he is too cute and delicate. We have missed each other and promise to write.

While in Montreal, I learn that my mother has had and survived uterine cancer. She has sold her rooming house on St. Andre and lives in an apartment in Verdun. She works as a saleswoman in a clothing store on Wellington Street. After recovering from her cancer, she bought a car and went to Ohio with my grandmother Rose to visit her brother Oliva. She doesn't have a driver's license, but after all she had driven the family tractor on the farm in her youth! As always, she is a daring and determined woman. Sadly, I return to Toronto without having seen her; she is so stubborn.

At work I am experiencing some conflict with Donna the chief accountant. She is good looking and has a rich American lover who lives in Buffalo, New York with his family but visits her on weekends. She wears expensive, store-bought dresses, goes to the hairdresser, gets facials, and snubs me from her pedestal. She is difficult to work with, and I complain to the controller, Walter. He is particularly fond of me and calls her into his office. She comes out in tears but strangely enough we will become long-lasting friends. Walter, who hired me, stole my heart the moment he bent down low by my side to explain to me something he wanted done. I dislike weekends when I cannot see him, and I wait by the office window to watch him arrive at the office on Monday mornings. Of course, he is unaware of my feelings for him. He has a very elegant wife and a baby boy. It is complete folly on my part, and I know it.

Meanwhile in Montreal, Monic tries to convince my mother to welcome us to her Christmas party. We arrive in the middle of the party. My mother has had a few drinks already, and she welcomes us with a smile. Strangely, she seems comfortable enough with Paul. Everything is going fine until Paul, rightfully, feels abandoned while I spend too much time in conversation with Denis. Back at the hotel, we fight and return quickly to Toronto—with every letter I receive from Denis, he grumbles. Paul is starting to get on my nerves.

I believe it is best for everyone if I look for another job. I join an advertising agency. Molly, a pretty and vivacious brunette, shows me how to do the payroll. Al teaches me how to keep a small set of books for his private company. I learn fast, work hard, and get regular increases in salary. I love my work, and I'm becoming more and more independent. Paul feels he is losing me and starts looking elsewhere. He decides to take up golfing and spends a lot of time at it. With more time alone, I buy a guitar and teach myself how to play a few chords from a method-teaching book. I also take painting lessons and start decorating the walls with my efforts. Paul is away every weekend afternoon and often in the evenings. *Is golf is keeping him that busy?* I decide to test him. I take the putter out of his golf bag ... and he doesn't notice a thing. I know that he is cheating on me, and I start thinking of leaving him.

In 1967, it's Expo in Montreal. Paul encourages me to go up there for a few days. My mother and Aunt Olida receive me in turn. I go out with Denis to a gay bar on Crescent Street. I find the women quite sexy and exciting, and I secretly dream of returning.

Back home, a neighbour stops me and tells me that while I was away, Paul had a woman in our apartment. I also find a powder compact by the bathroom sink. I confront Paul; he says that he let a friend from work and his girlfriend use our apartment as a favour. She must have forgotten it there. I am just waiting for the right moment to leave him without feeling guilty. I return to Montreal frequently. Denis and I go dancing in gay bars. He does not have a serious lover yet. He goes out with friends, never alone: he could get beaten by some homophobic thugs or caught up in a police raid.

In 1968, one afternoon after work, I get home to find a woman sitting in my living room waiting for me. Paul's face is grey; he looks pitiful. She tells me she needs $400 for an abortion: she is pregnant with a second child from Paul. My immediate reaction is to ask her "Where is the first one?" Her little boy has been in foster homes since his birth on February 21, 1966. She quickly understands that I want to adopt him. She thinks that the Children's Social Service Center will never allow me to adopt him. I wonder why she has not kept her baby. She tells me that it is because raising a bi-racial child is too difficult in this society … but why get pregnant a second time? Despite her having been my husband's mistress for a few years I feel no animosity towards her. In fact, I feel sorry for her. All my efforts are aimed at adopting this child. Paul is not too keen about it, but he is willing to adopt his own son, nevertheless. We get custody of Shane Anthony in October. What a good-looking child he is and so darn intelligent. He clings to me but not to Paul. He pushes away any other child that approaches me. When a social worker comes to check on him after two weeks, Shane quickly presents her coat to her so that she may leave.

Shane stutters and seems to fear people. I sing "Summertime" to him at bedtime. Soon, he sings the last word of every phrase with me. At daycare he makes scenes. I am not thinking of leaving Paul anymore because I think he is happy and settled with his little family. I am not even worried when I find out that Anne, Shane's mother, works at the same office as he does.

At the beginning of December, the company where they work offers a Christmas party to the families of its employees. When we arrive Anne spontaneously comes to her son. She is thrilled, but I am uncomfortable. Upon returning home I get a phone call from her telling me that Paul still rings her doorbell. I say nothing, I want Shane to have a good Christmas.

I contact Donna, my friend from the advertising company in Don Mills. I have not seen her for quite a while. We meet, and I have a shock when I see her. She has a little daughter, Shanna. Donna looks impoverished and drives a beaten-up car. Her rich boyfriend did not acknowledge paternity and abandoned her. I tell her what has happened to me and that I am planning to move before the New Year. She proposes that we share an apartment. I agree and reserve the movers for 9 a.m. on December 28, after Paul has left for work and Shane is at daycare. I leave my new address on the kitchen counter so that Paul can continue to see his son.

We move onto the first floor of a duplex on Queen Street. Donna occupies the master bedroom, the children the small room and I sleep in the living room where I can enjoy the electric fireplace. We are just a few steps from the boardwalk by Lake Ontario. It is a delightful place to live. I find a job downtown at an electric company. I am the receptionist, secretary and accountant. I earn a particularly good salary and I am free. I take Shane to Montreal to visit Lea; she thinks it was a bad idea for me to adopt him. I guess I must have given her a tough time.

After a few months of the children bickering, I decide to move back to Montreal. I find a small apartment downtown. I am twenty-nine-years old, and I am returning to the Belle Province after ten years. The movers let me sit in between them with Shane on my lap. After finding a babysitter for Shane, I find work at another advertising agency. I have experience in the field, and I have good references. I have my eye on a young copywriter named Gilles Ouellette; I enjoy that he flirts with me. We have different political views: I am a liberal and he is a separatist. I follow him to a FLQ protest, and he tells me to speak quietly as I have a bit of an English accent from hardly having spoken French for ten years. His friends are all bearded pseudo-intellectual types. It is new and fun for me.

One day, I come back from work to find that someone has broken into my apartment and stolen the few things I have. I am scared to stay there now. Gilles invites me and Shane to go live with him on Fabre Street while I find somewhere else to live. I must find another babysitter for Shane, and I find a pearl: Mrs. Guay lives on Garnier Street, the very street where I want to move eventually. Shane takes to her quickly, and his French improves daily but he still stutters. Gilles receives François Boucher, a camera operator at a Quebec film and television production company. He is just in from an assignment abroad and has a lot of interesting tales to tell. We smoke a little marijuana and a current pass between him, and I. Gilles is not offended; he likes me but is not in love with me. He is awaiting the return of his past girlfriend and the child he had with her.

Spring arrives and I leave Gilles' house to occupy a small apartment nearby. I furnish it with the bare minimum. I don't care for my current job and find another one on Ste. Catherine Street as an accountant for publishers of articles on the cultural events in Montreal.

I have a press membership card that allows me to assist at various premieres. I love the environment.

One of my colleagues Elspeth Moore, is a young girl from Westmount. She has a monthly allowance larger than her salary! She spends most of her time on the phone planning her weekend social events. She is very generous with me; on my birthday she offers me an expensive bottle of champagne and treats me to a restaurant where I learn how to eat artichokes. Also, there is Al, the young artist who designs the front pages of the magazine. I often smoke a little pot with him and his boyfriend during lunch hours. I happen to open my purse next to a nosy girl at the office—she sees a little bag of pot and runs up to the president of the company, who fires me on the spot. My immediate supervisor (who smokes also) cannot do anything.

I meet my cousin Denis; he now lives with Yannick on Ste. Catherine Street near Drummond. There's a vacant apartment across from theirs; he convinces me to rent it. I am without a job, and the rent is double what I am paying now, but what the heck, I go for it! Mrs. Guay will look after Shane during the week from now on; she loves to pamper him. I meet an interviewer at a placement agency. She says I have good face and my resume is good. I always find a good excuse for being without a job. There is an opening at a slipper manufacturer in the east end of town. Mr. Gadoury, a Hungarian immigrant, receives me. He is the surly type and before leaving I ask him if he is always so grumpy. He hires me.

Mr. Gadoury always eats his lunch in his office, never goes out at noon, and always has that sullen look on his face. It is lunchtime and I ask him to come out and eat with me. To my surprise he gets up off his chair and follows me; we become quite good friends. I now call him Julius. He takes me to watch football games at Jarry Park where he has front-seat tickets. He frequents gay bars; he is a peculiar fellow, maybe a bit of a voyeur. He knows the staff at a popular cabaret on St. Andre Street. I am with him, and he points out a young tomboy to me. She works as a busboy, emptying ashtrays and wiping tables. He knows her well and is going to hire her next week. Come Monday, he calls me into his office and introduces me to Kim. I must sit with her to gather the necessary information to put her on the payroll. I am blushing because of what goes on in my head! The same evening Julius invites both of us to his penthouse for supper.

II

Kim is nineteen-years old; her parents live in Embrun, not far from the Ontario border. She left her parents' house at seventeen. She has already visited Canada from coast to coast hidden in freight trains. During these trips, she stopped at orchards and farms to work for a few months at a time. I go to visit her. She has a room where the daughter of a renowned mafioso lives, in a shady part of town—that girl is a permanent sight at the cabaret. She has a diamond encrusted in one of her front teeth. She is surrounded by a group of girls that she pimps. It is not a place for Kim to live in, and I invite her to come and live with me. My life will change dramatically! Sadly, Denis does not like her. Kim is my first female partner. I must introduce her to my mother. I invite Lea for supper and tell her that I'm taking a break from men for now. She is okay with that.

Donna, who I call from time to time, wants to attend classes at McGill University and decides to move to Montreal. She moves to the suburb of Longueuil with her daughter Shanna. My new orientation doesn't bother her if everyone knows that *she* is not like that. She befriends my Aunt Olida and becomes quite attached to her.

I am still working at the slipper factory, and I take home a lot of samples that Julius gives me. The Greenberg brothers are partners with Julius—they falsely accuse me of stealing from them. I throw my pencil at them and tell them where to stick it. I leave before they can fire me. Julius calls me later and asks me how I could have left him alone with those bandits. He takes care of all the paperwork necessary for me to get unemployment insurance. We still get together from time to time, Julius, Kim, and I.

When I am thirty, Kim offers me a little grey and white kitty. I call him Artemis. After having to search for employment, I join a realty company. Looking at their books, I soon realize that they are on the brink of bankruptcy as the cash flow barely covers the payroll. I work for Peter; he is younger than I. He is a new-age type of fellow. He keeps in touch with members of a sect in Alexandria, Ontario. He doesn't seem to worry much about anything. He believes that life shows us the right choices to make at the right time; no need to worry in advance. He fascinates me in some ways.

He proposes that we go with him, Shane and I, to visit his friends at the community. The followers live and work on a large farm. The women occupy the top floor of the large house and the men, the main floor. Everyone speaks quietly and in a low voice. They share everything. The leader of the sect takes care of the finances. After a group meeting and a good supper, we return to Montreal. It is raining very hard; Highway 401 is very slippery. Peter is driving too fast; we hydroplane and go off the road, through the guard rail. Everything happens very fast. The hood of the car contracts like an accordion bellows, and the impact throws us through the windshield. We land unconscious in a field. When I come to, kind people are holding a tarpaulin over Shane and me. I hear sirens coming from afar. I try to get up, but I am prevented from doing so: I have a broken clavicle and less serious injuries to a wrist and knee. Shane also has a broken clavicle as well and has a bump on the head. Peter stands stoically, his hand on a few broken ribs. In the ambulance, Shane looks at me and says, "Mom, your face is all dirty" … and this without stuttering. He will never stutter again.

Shane heals very quickly, and so do I, but while I am recuperating, I need a little help when Kim is at work. She calls my mother and tells her what happened. Lea answers, "No wonder, with the life she leads." It is Aunt Olida who comes to visit and help me. I return to work after a few weeks. I don't know for how long because the firm has filed for bankruptcy. Peter advises me to seek compensation from his insurance, and I follow his advice.

Donna calls us. She wants us to go with her to look at the plans of a housing project in Brossard, a Montreal suburb. The three-bedroom bungalows will sell for $15,000. I have $500 saved up for an eventual vacation. The occupancy is projected for early 1971. Donna is not sure, but I go for it and put down my $500 as a deposit. What a great thing I think I am doing for my family! Kim is furious: how dare I make such a decision without consulting her? I have made my first mistake with her. Monic and Andrew, Denis and Yannick also buy a house in the same neighbourhood. We all move there in spring of 1971. We need a car to get around. Kim gets her driving permit and buys a hatchback. She now works for a transport company.

Peter tells me that the realty company is closing their doors. It's the first time I cry about losing a job. I loved working for that dreamy young man! I find another job in a hurry; I have mortgage payments and taxes to pay. I land a bookkeeping job at the head office Cyber-medic a private clinic that analyzes medical check-up results by computer. They have several branches. Working on consolidation at the end of the month is complex for me: it is high time I get a diploma in accounting. I sign up for the CGA (Chartered

General Accountant) correspondence course, but first I must take the year-end exams at HEC Montreal (High Commercial Studies of Montreal).

We move to our new house in the spring of 1971. The landscaping has yet to be done, and there is mud everywhere. Despite Kim's grumbling, I am ecstatic. My mother also has moved from Verdun to Montreal, to an apartment block on Bercy Street. The appliances are included in her lease, so she sells me her beautiful copper-toned fridge and stove. She is very happy there; it's modern and has an outdoor swimming pool. She also has a weekend lover, Jean-Jacques Dubuc. She is in great mood. I ask her to lend me $600 to pay for my divorce from Paul. I get my divorce quickly as I am not asking for alimony.

Once installed in my house, I buy an old upright piano painted blue which I put in our bedroom. Kim doesn't appreciate my playing, neither does she like me studying all the time. Our immediate neighbours are very nice but around the crescent there is much gossip: poor little boy living with two women! The backyard neighbour snubs us. One morning as I am sitting in the bus on my way to work, I see him getting on. As soon as he approaches my level, I stretch my leg a wee bit to the side, with a result you can guess. I get great satisfaction from seeing him trip.

I receive a compensation cheque from the insurance company. With that $5,000, the first thing I buy is a colour television. It's the latest thing. Shane inherits the black and white one for his room. He spends a lot of time glued to it. I have a large swimming pool dug up in the back yard. The neighbours' children watch through their fence at "poor little" Shane splashing happily in his pool. I warn Shane that no new friends are allowed in, only the old ones. We have a great summer. Kim invites a colleague from her office; she teaches me how to dive. I am afraid of deep water, but as soon as I dive in six feet, I go back up four feet, so I quickly overcome my fear.

Kim and I live like any normal family. My relatives live close to us, my friend Donna is in Longueuil (a suburb next to ours), and we have two cats: Artemis and a grey Siamese called Sam. I am getting along better with my mother. Shane goes to school and afterwards awaits my return from work at his friend Eric's. I pay his mother, Mrs. Labonte, a few dollars a week for this service.

The following summer, Mother, Shane, Kim, and I go camping down in Ogunquit, Maine. When I see the Atlantic Ocean, I am overwhelmed by its beauty and swear to come again. Back to work I find my job too demanding and with my newly acquired skills I start looking at job offers in the newspapers. A social service centre in Westmount has a post advertised. They need an accountant and offer a very good salary. I apply, and in one swoop my annual salary goes up by $4,000 per year with more adjustments to the salary scale to come.

It's a real sinecure; I supervise the payroll clerk and take care of the books. Chantale Knight is the centre's secretary. She lives with her girlfriend as I do. We spend our lunch hours together and after a while we welcome one another into our homes.

I have money to spare and dream of traveling. As a surprise gift to Kim and Shane, I plan a trip to the Bahamas for the three of us: my second mistake. How could I do this without consulting her beforehand? I am much too impulsive, I guess. From now on I will travel with Olida, Monic, and Mom. We will go to Cuba and take a cruise in the Caribbean.

By summer 1975, Kim no longer wants to be with us. She moves to Ottawa with a neighbour's wife. I watch her load a small truck with her stuff and some of mine even some of my clothes. I am sad to see her go but that's life. What can I do? A few weeks later, I see that the neighbour's wife is back. She is rocking her daughter on their porch, wearing some of my clothes. Kim does not return. Six months pass, and I put up the house for sale. The real estate agent tells me I have a hatchback dressed up like a sedan. Nevertheless, he finds a buyer, and I accept an offer of $35,500—not a bad deal. Meanwhile, Kim has returned to Brossard and bought herself a house much bigger and fancier than mine. She suggests that we move in with her ... but no thank you, I'm moving back to Montreal!

On June 19, 1976, Shane and I move into a beautiful two-bedroom apartment in Côte-St-Luc. I still have my blue piano and my two cats. I buy new living room and dining room furniture. Shane is ten years old; he still spends his time in his room watching television. He no longer wants to have a babysitter. He is very serious for his age.

The head office of the Center has moved to a new location in the former Place Dupuis building. Chantale continues to work at the Westmount office while I am moved to the new office where I become the assistant to the Director of Finance, Harvey. He is easygoing, not too bossy, and appreciates my work. We talk a lot; he likes music, and his favourite singer is Olivia Newton John. I like Donna Summer, Supertramp, and Fleetwood Mac. We go to lunch together on Fridays.

Denis tells me to get a car, so I do not have to depend on people for a ride. He is right, and I do have my driver's license but not much experience. I buy a little mustard-yellow Datsun, three-and-a-half horsepower. It is straight out of the showroom, and they must get it ready for me to pick up the next day. I use it to visit my mother, run errands, and go to gay bars on Saturday nights. Since I do not see from my right eye, I am always scared to drive, I hate it.

Barely a month since I have moved here, Kim sells her house and moves into the same building I live in. *Whatever was she thinking?* However, she ignores me when we meet in the elevator and does not appear to have found a new partner.

Shane and I join my relatives for a Christmas Eve feast at Denis and Yannick's apartment on St. Urbain Street. It is in a century-old building with the original stone walls. Lynda, Monic, and Andrew's daughter bring a layered bread filled with pâté, eggs, and cheese, wrapped up in cream cheese. It tastes great. We have a fun time. Earlier that day, Kim had knocked on our door bearing gifts … I bid her goodbye and closed the door. That was the end of this episode of my life.

On December 26, 1976, Chantale and her new girlfriend, Claudette Desbiens, suggest that we meet later in the evening at Gillie's a gay bar for women. At 9 p.m., I am sitting alone at a table waiting for them. There is this good-looking young girl sitting alone at the bar quietly smoking a cigarette. I find her attractive, and I approach the empty stool next to her. I ask if it is okay for me to sit there while I am waiting for some friends. I introduce myself, and she offers me a cigarette. I am not a smoker, but I take one anyway to save face. We even dance a little. Her name is Ginette Dubuc. After a while, I invite her to join me at my table and while we wait for my friends, we have an enjoyable conversation. She is twenty-five years old and still lives with her parents. I can tell she is a good person, and I would like to get to know her better; she as well thinks that we could be together, perhaps for a long time. I like her a lot already!

My friends Chantale and Claudette join us. We chat, dance, and have a few drinks. It is one of many great evenings we will spend together the four of us. I propose that we end the evening at my place. Our three cars follow one another on Cavendish Boulevard. I am excited; I make them bacon and tomato sandwiches with mayonnaise. Ginette eats hers without saying anything, even though she does not like mayonnaise. She is tired; she has three jobs: one full time at a bank and two others part time at a performing arts venue and at Jarry Park. She sleeps in and goes home the next day. She barely sees Shane at breakfast before he runs back to his room.

During the week, we go to the cinema to see the movie *Lucky Luke* with Shane and Patrick, Ginette's nephew. Patrick is fascinated to hear me speak to Shane in English. He is a bright and cheerful little boy; he quickly gets attached to Shane and we spend a lovely afternoon. On New Year's Eve, Ginette arrives in her orange Camaro wearing her wildcat fur coat. She is impressive! She offers me a Nicole Croisille album and one by the pianist André Gagnon. She has also a bottle of expensive red wine. In addition to being pretty, she is generous, and she loves my cats. Sadly, Shane is sulky; he is too possessive of me.

On New Year's Day 1977, Ginette returns to her parent's apartment for lunch and tells them that she is moving in with a girlfriend. There's great consternation in the household. It is especially hard for Marguerite, who saw her daughter as her old age support. Ginette brings very little with her: some clothing and a few books. She has records of Aznavour and Reggiani—a little too sad for my taste but I don't care. We meet Kim in the elevator; her eyes are as big as saucers when she sees who I am with. I can see the envy in her eyes, and I feel so proud. Ginette picks me up after work, and I ride in her orange sports car. She thinks my little car is a joke but one day she will sell the Camaro and buy my Datsun which she will pay for when she can. She must get rid of some debts and stop working at three jobs.

Another birthday, my mother invites me to her apartment to celebrate the occasion. It is my opportunity to introduce Ginette to her. It's a mutual admiration society. Those two Virgos get along well. My mother's boyfriend, Jean-Jacques Dubuc, is there too. What a coincidence, mother and daughter both have lovers named Dubuc! Monic knows Jean-Jacques well, they used to work at the same law firm where she was a switchboard operator. His nephew is a lawyer at the firm; he calls Jean-Jacques "uncle." Everyone calls Jean-Jacques "uncle" in the office, so does Monic. He becomes "uncle" to us, as well. What an elegant, refined, and attentive gentleman. No wonder my mother fell for him. She met him at a law firm when she worked there a few nights as a cleaning lady, dusting desks. She was waiting at the bus stop on her way home while he stood in line behind her. He recognized her, started a conversation, and invited her for a drink. From then on, she always wore a fancy dress under her apron when she went to work there on Friday nights.

Aunt Olida, having lost her husband Conrad in a car accident a while back, now lives with Romeo Pilon in Fabreville. He is a friendly and amusing widower who she met at a club called The Eagles. It is a good place to drink, dance, and meet people. We are invited for supper; she makes her famous spicy chicken spaghetti. Denis is there, and he who disliked Kim so much is enthralled by Ginette. They become great friends.

I do not renew my lease; I am dreaming of owning a house again. I ask Ginette if she would be interested in buying a house with me. She still has too many debts and refuses. I buy a row house on MacMahon Street in Notre-Dame-de-Grâce. We have three bedrooms upstairs and a large living room on the main floor with a dining-room next to the kitchen. There is a garage below with a sloping entrance. It looks good; the living-room has red wall-to-wall carpet, and I make macrame curtains for the dining room. We have a large white melamine shelf leaning against the back wall filled with records and books, and there is built-in lighting. I am so proud of our home! I invite my boss Harvey over so that he can meet Ginette. He already knows I live with a woman.

One time, there's a knock at the door. A handsome man is standing there, who asks to see his daughter. I finally meet Ginette's dad. He is very nice; we share a Scotch and a beer, and he leaves satisfied that his daughter is comfortable and happy. Place-des-Arts presents a Ginette Reno concert, and I meet Ginette's mother for the first time. She is a pretty woman; she too realizes that I present no danger to her daughter. We attend the performance together. We invite Ginette's parents to dinner at our house, and for the same occasion we invite Jacques Plante, the former goaltender for the Canadiens, with his wife Raymonde. They are friends of Ginette. They met at Jarry Park when Raymonde was Ginette's supervisor. She has travelled with them across Canada and to Boston during hockey season. If there was a little ice left to melt between Marguerite and I, it is done.

Shane goes to English school. Sadly, some boys tease him because of me; there's even a neighbour that rings our doorbell to tell us that we are misfits in the neighbourhood. It so happens that Denis comes by and talks about some friends of his that have just bought a century-old house on Lusignan Street, between St. Antoine and St. Jacques Street. These former grey stone duplexes narrowly escaped demolition during the construction of the Ville-Marie Expressway. These are now used as rooms for rent, by the week. It is a very poor neighbourhood. Around the corner there's the Welcome Hall Mission where the homeless can get a free meal. There are two side-by-side duplexes for sale there, at the ridiculous price of $15,000 for both. Of course, there is considerable work to be done for them to be habitable. It is a godsend, and I grab the opportunity.

Sadly, I must let the roomers go. We rent containers and fill them with the plaster and grit we remove from the walls. The basement ceiling is rotten, and we have it taken down; it is filled with soot that falls on the workers' heads. Old beds and kitchen furniture are discarded as well. We keep several small antique pieces of furniture that we will strip later. We do a lot of work ourselves during the weekend, and when we return to our home on MacMahon Street at the end of the day, we undress in the portico so as not to dirty the house. My hairdresser asks me what's my line of work when she sees the plaster glued to my scalp.

Ginette brushes every brick visible on the walls and cleans them with muriatic acid. We strip the interior staircase that leads to the upper duplex. These houses have two duplexes, one on top of the other. We will rent the basement and main floors and occupy the second and third floors. We hire a company to sand and varnish the beautiful Colombian pine floorboards. The plumbing and electricity must be redone completely, the kitchens and bathrooms as well. My mother advances me the necessary funds, with interest of course. We have two new front doors installed and hire two carpenters to install the door handles. One is tall and one is short. They drill the holes according to their own heights. A second hole must be drilled to realign them, and brass plates purchased and installed to hide their error. It is a great apartment with its ten-foot ceilings, brick walls, and beautiful blond floors. There are large French windows, with the panes closing on each other in the middle. We have a lot of light as the dining room communicates with the living room through a large opening on the wall, and the windows are at both ends.

We sell the house on MacMahon and move to Lusignan Street on September 9, 1978. It's Ginette's birthday. The first evening we are treated to a birds-eye view of the showers at the Welcome Hall Mission. It doesn't last. I leave the piano on the ground floor to strip it before moving it to the second floor. Behind the blue layer, there is a brown layer, and the original varnish layer. I am starting to have asthma. We buy two beautiful large Turkish-type rugs, two dark-green couches with pale wooden arms, and a large maple cabinet to hold our 700 records and our sound system. We have a ceiling fan installed in the living room. There is a small office off this space where the piano will go. We still must replace the doors in the bedrooms upstairs as they are barely hanging from their century-old rotten frames. When the time comes to move the piano upstairs, it looks very good stripped down to the wood. We hire three muscular guys to move it upstairs, and halfway there, they drop it. The piano has a large crack in the back, and there is a note that will no longer resonate.

We often receive our friends and relatives for meals at our large wooden table, which we bought from an antique shop. That summer we have a ten-by-ten balcony built at the rear, overlooking a yard and a parking space. Denis and Marcel have a balcony next to ours; it is very convenient. On their side, work is progressing more slowly. Denis is a fine artist but earns very little; Marcel is a hairdresser in Westmount. He receives good tips but must pay for all the expenses alone. He even leaves Denis twenty dollars every day for pocket money.

We rent the downstairs duplex to Lucy, a teacher. She is delighted. There is a small wood fireplace in her living room and a parking place at the back. I like the neighbourhood, there are blacks, gays, folks from Gaspe, Iran and poor people. There is always a line of homeless people waiting for the Mission Hall to open for meals. Everyone minds their own business. Harvey, my boss, comes to see us. He is curious to see what we have accomplished. He meets my cousin Denis—I think he is secretly attracted by his bohemian demeanour. If he could, he would hire him to paint a mural in the entrance hall of the offices.

On the other side of the party wall of Denis' apartment there is another house like ours but with an ancient Finnish steam sauna. It is for sale. Denis convinces his mother Olida to buy it. She and Romeo leave Fabreville to settle near us. At sixty-seven-years old, my aunt is learning how to control the steam pressure as well as receiving clients; she lets Denis know when there's a good-looking guy alone in one of the saunas. Olida and Romeo have installed their living room and kitchen in the basement where they have a big fireplace; their bedroom is on the main floor. So here we are: three houses in a row inhabited by relatives! We have a great time playing cards, drinking Cutty Sark and singing. I always have my guitar with me so I can play a few chords to accompany us. The street is slowly gentrifying.

Our friends Chantale and Claudette don't live very far from us, on Saint-Jacques near Monkland Street. Chantale often mentions her friend Yvon to us. He is the Human Resources Director at the Hilton airport hotel. On the eve of my thirty-ninth birthday, they invite us to their house; I have a bad cold, but we go anyway. They introduce us to Yvon Belair and his partner Roger Gagne. These guys are adorable.

We are invited to their apartment in Ville LaSalle. Nice decor, good ambiance; they have the fireplace going and Ravel's "Bolero" playing in a loop. Yvon is a fine cook; he has studied at the Quebec Hotel and Tourism Institute. We develop a strong friendship. We are often invited to spend a night in a fine room of the hotel after a fancy supper in the dining-room. Yvon is an amusing guy; he makes me laugh, especially when he imitates the singing Indian accent. Roger is introverted, but he loosens up after a few drinks. These two young men really complement each other. Chantale and Claudette are buying the top floor of a triplex in Notre-Dame-de-Grace, and one of their acquaintances is buying the main floor. The second floor is available, and I encourage Yvon and Roger to buy it. Yvon is only twenty-five and a bit nervous, but I prod him a little, and he goes for it. They become homeowners for the first time but not the last. They will later buy a duplex on St. Hubert Street.

Meanwhile, back home, Shane worries me. At thirteen, he doesn't have any friends, and he doesn't come out of his room when we have friends over. He leaves for school before I get up and has made his own supper by the time I come home from work. He is very independent, and I respect his privacy.

While he is away and has left his bedroom door open, I notice on his desk a list of choices: "stay or go." I am intrigued and look at it more closely. Under leaving, the list is long but under staying he has noted only, "but I love my mother." I am very moved. There is friction between him and Ginette. Shane makes faces at her when my back is turned. Ginette confides in Denis, who tells her that she should leave. It hurts me to see her go. I cry a lot, and Shane tells me not to worry, she will come back. He doesn't seem to realize that it is his fault. But he is right, she does return after a few days. She had gone to Chantale and Claudette's to get pampered a little.

At work there is something going on: there are analysts and programmers all around and talk of computers. I do payroll and accounting by hand … I can see the end coming. They implement the programs that will take over these tasks. The Director of Finance and I are no longer needed. After six years with them, I am ready for a change.

On my fortieth birthday, Ginette and Denis surprise me with this great party at Denis' place next door. There are streamers and balloons hanging from the rafters, and they have borrowed a few candles from the Notre Dame Basilica to set the mood. Marguerite, Ginette's mother, has prepared a splendid buffet. Everyone brings their own bottle of champagne or sparkling wine. Shane, Mom and her boyfriend, Monic, Andrew and Lynda, Olida and Romeo, and a few other friends are there. Denis plays "Staying Alive" by the Bee Gees to get the dancing going. It's a great party! Spring is here, and there are streamers all the way down the street.

My curriculum vitae updated; I go to an employment agency. They send me to a small law firm located in Place Victoria. I am interviewed by Mr. Saul Semple Esquire. He asks me what I have been told about lawyers; I answer honestly that I was told that they are all primadonnas. Mr. Semple stands up suddenly, turns his back to me, looks out the window, takes a couple of deep breaths, and sits back down. I have just insulted one of the top guys of the firm! I get the position with the wacky title of Comptroller, but I control absolutely nothing. After five years, the firm grows exponentially. They move into two upper floors of Place Ville-Marie. They hire a Director of Finance and install computers … I am out of a job again.

Denis and Marcel put their house up for sale as they cannot find the necessary funds to complete the renovations. The house sold; they move to a large apartment building on Peel Street. They have an extraordinary view of the city. The rent is expensive, and they start fighting over money. Marcel is fed up with being the only breadwinner; he leaves Denis. My cousin had just turned thirty-five in October of 1981, and we send him a card showing an astronaut waving to people before going into a spaceship. Denis doesn't see himself as handsome, though he still is—with one eye mainly blue with a bit of brown and the other mainly brown with a touch of blue. He still has a devastating personality.

One night, in April 1982, Denis snorts cocaine, drinks champagne, takes too many pills, writes a parting later naming each of us, and passes away. At the funeral home, Marcel lays a bouquet of red roses in his coffin—a year later he will jump off the Jacques Cartier Bridge. Aunt Olida must empty the apartment and surprisingly, finds on the floor the birthday card we'd sent Denis, with showing the astronaut. It is as if he is telling us not to worry, that he is leaving for a great journey. She keeps his great watercolours, and I inherit his drawing table that no one wants. It is such a sad place now that the next-door neighbour is a stranger.

Shane, at seventeen, is a ghost in the house; I can't stand it. I go with him on several occasions to meet a social worker. The last time she tells him, "So what did you do to punish your mother this week?" In agreement with Ginette, I call Jacqueline Pilon and put the house up for sale. She is a very elegant and well-spoken lady. She finds buyers who sign an offer to purchase for $85,000. The next day, after having toured the neighbourhood, they cancel their offer to purchase. We accept someone else's offer at $75,000. Ginette and I both work for the same law firm, and one of the perks is free counsel. We take the people who didn't honour their contract to court, and we recover the $10,000 difference.

I repay the loan I owed my mother, and I get a mortgage to buy a five-plex on Laurier Street near Papineau. I find a small apartment for Shane in Ville St. Laurent. I give him a series of cheques to cover his monthly rent and groceries up to his eighteenth birthday. He will send me his hydro bill. Romeo moves him in his van. It is a heart-wrenching decision to make, but it's my life or his. I love Shane, but I love me more.

We occupy the main floor of the new place and start making some renovations. Starting with the kitchen, we replace the back door with a patio door and fixed windows on each side. The kitchen now has wall-to-wall windows that face the back yard. We strip the floor and have it sanded before installing the new cupboards and the stand-alone counter with its cook top. In the back yard there is a shed that we demolish, we cover the ground with turf. With a table, chairs, and a red-and-white parasol, it becomes a little paradise. The children next door spy on us through the fence, and one neighbour listens to his soccer games at full volume while sitting on his balcony. But we can live with that for a while.

The dining room has beautiful mouldings, up and down; there is a beautiful rosette around the chandelier, and the floors are already in great shape. We paint the mouldings and the rosette a glossy white and the walls midnight blue. We buy from a high-end furniture store a white lacquered table and buffet; the six white chairs have dark blue cushions. The floor is almost completely covered with one of our imitation red Turkish rugs. In a corner stands an array of red lacquered twigs in a large white plant pot. The rest of the floor we leave as is, there is a divided double room, the front part for the living-room and the back part we use as an office. Most apartments around here are divided the same way, and most people use the back part as a bedroom.

Ginette takes Chinese cooking classes with friends from work: Sylvie, Manon, and Lucie. They come to our place to prepare a superb Hong Kong-style meal. They laugh a lot and are having a real good time while they chop and sip martinis. Ginette also tests her new talent on her brother Robert and his wife Francine; she makes them dumplings and Beggar's' Chicken—that's a skinless chicken wrapped in dough.

After ten months, Ginette sees a cockroach climbing up the party wall. We call Jacqueline, our real estate agent. A young couple come over with a friend who happens to be an interior decorator. After a few days, they present us with an acceptable offer to purchase ... but there's a slight problem: they have a lease. They live in a tiny basement apartment on de Bullion Street near Prince Arthur Street. No problem! We put our furniture in storage and move into their studio. We pay the rent to them, and they pay the proprietor, who never knows the difference.

We buy a sofa bed and use our garden furniture in the kitchen corner. We keep our parasol opened for the heck of it. We have access to the backyard, and we buy a lawnmower that cuts the grass by hovering over it. We store it in an unlocked shed, and you guessed it—the flying mower flew away, never to be found again. There are thieves everywhere. While we live there, we frequent the Greek restaurants where one can bring their own wine. There is also a Chinese restaurant where we become friends with the owner. We have New Year's Day lunch there with Jacqueline.

I get a phone call from Shane's landlord. He hasn't paid his rent for three months, even though he has graduated and could have found himself a job. I tell his landlord that Shane has a father and give him Paul's phone number. Paul comes down to Montreal and brings Shane back to live with he and his wife in Toronto. He will meet his two half-sisters and find himself a job.

Ginette and I get into the habit of going to Memphremagog Beach on Sundays, often with Yvon and Roger and at times with my mother. Windsurfing is the latest thing, and Ginette buys a windsurfing board. We must get it out through the basement window and install it on the roof of our little hatchback. Everyone has a go at it, Jean-Paul, Ginette's father, Yvon, Roger, and me.

Ginette even goes windsurfing at Lac Saint-Jean where Roger's parents live. It is a big lake, she gets disoriented for a moment, but good souls steer her back to port. My Ginette is so brave, she even skydives in Valcourt with a young lawyer from the office as I and her parents watch with our hearts in our heels.

I get a call from Veronica Doherty, Mr. Byer's secretary. He is on the board of directors at a Montreal bank. Aware of an opening in the trust department, he asks Veronica to call me so that I may apply. I do, and I start the next day. This job falls from the sky! It is most interesting, and I get the drift of it very quickly.

Jacqueline suggests that we buy a triplex on Cherrier Street. This time Ginette is willing to invest with me, and we buy it together. We sell the first and third floors and occupy the second floor. We change the windows for the identical model that we had on Lusignan and have new kitchen cupboards installed. We have the sloping floors sanded. In the bathroom we change the toilet, the sink, and the shower. Sadly, for me there is no bathtub. We move in as soon as the lease is terminated on de Bullion Street.

One fine Sunday during a trip to Magog, we walk by a promoter that has a layout of a condo project next to the lake. Mr. Beauvais seems respectable, and I trust him. It is a great project and I opt for a condo with a mezzanine. It should be ready by next summer. We must pay in installments as it goes up.

I love being near water, and every summer we go down to Ogunquit. Yvon often invites us to spend an afternoon by the airport hotel's swimming pool. When he is on duty as director, some weekends we have a fancy supper with he and Roger: champagne, oysters, good wine and port, good food, the works. To top it off, we stay overnight at one of the hotel's finest rooms. I guess by now Chantale and Claudette are getting a bit jealous! Yvon also has free accommodation benefits wherever this hotel chain is located, so together we go to Quebec City, Boston, New York, and even to Cartagena in Colombia. Yvon speaks good Spanish, on top of English and French. He even must go down to Cuba to train the staff at one of Cuba's new Hilton hotel chains.

Back home, tired of walking on slanting floors, we start looking for condos for sale on the south shore. There is a new development in St. Lambert de Navarre Street; one condo is for sale on a top floor with a mezzanine. We prepare an informal offer to purchase even before seeing the apartment. The vendor seems very eager to sell and accepts our offer without negotiating. Three days after we move, we hear that he was blown up in his car.

Mr. Beauvais asks me for an initial $15,000 as soon as construction begins. We go down to Magog with my mother, Yvon, and Roger to check the work in progress and by the same token enjoy a swim and a picnic.

At the Bank's fiduciary department, we learn the trade on the spot. Mr. Gaston Cantin, a notary for the firm, is transferred in from the Quebec City branch to give us courses on estate settlements. He is the absolute intellectual type with glasses and a little beard. He teaches very well, and I get promoted to the estates division. We get to talk from time to time. The ladies in the cubicles next to mine smoke non-stop; my asthma gets worse. Everyone in my life smokes while I am coughing my lungs out!

Mr. Beauvais asks me for a second $15,000 as the walls are starting to go up.

Yvon and Roger buy a condo on de Navarre, next to ours. It is not to Roger's taste however; he would rather live in a house, but Yvon is compulsive like me and often moves too fast. As neighbours, we see each other a lot and go to Magog together often. Roger wants to live in a house, and St. Lambert is so beautiful. In my opinion, it is the best place to live on the south shore, if you can afford it. They quickly sell their condo to a fellow who pays in cash; they buy a nice bungalow on Alexandra Street. It has a swimming pool at the back, a garden and flower beds—everything Roger could dream of. We envy them a little; it is very comfortable in their backyard with the BBQ and the pool, and we love visiting there. Why couldn't we have the same? Of course, we do have the condo in Magog to pay for …

However, we do find a more modest house in Brossard on Boisclair Street. There is work to be done, but it is in our budget. We sell our condo and buy it. We start by removing the horrible wallpaper from the living room and dining room walls. It is an open-concept layout and once painted in the same white and dark-blue scheme of the house on Laurier Street, it looks pretty good—especially with the wooden beams across the ceiling. It has a fireplace that we cannot use because it smokes up the room, so we have one installed in the basement. The room downstairs has a patio door that opens on a backyard. It is enjoyable.

In Magog, the work seems to be slowing down, but I am asked to pay another $15,000. The project is built on marshland, and following a heavy rain, the basement floods.

The cost of this project is far exceeding the estimated budget. The promoter doesn't have the necessary funds to make up the deficit, and the Sicilian bank that finances the project withdraws and demands to be reimbursed. The Sicilian bank acquires the project in payment. We—the buyers—lose everything. We get together to form a committee to discuss what can be done. We agree on presenting an offer to purchase to the Sicilian bank. It is an attractive offer, but Mr. Beauvais, whom I trusted, with a group of architects and lawyers, present a higher bid than ours. The bank accepts their offer and rejects ours. We have no recourse; I have lost $45,000. I report the sad news to Ginette, Roger, Yvon, and my mother. They are so sorry for me. My mother is angry at the Blessed Virgin, to whom she had prayed so much. As for me, the saddest thing was to lose a beautiful dream.

Romeo, my aunt's boyfriend, has a small summer camp in Austin, near Magog. There are two small ponds where you can swim, if you are not too worried about crayfish. My Aunt Olida spends the summer there, and we visit them regularly. On one occasion we pass by a small chalet with a "For Sale" sign in the window. It is two trailers joined together and wrapped in a yellow vinyl covering. It sits on a quarter-acre of land. At the foot of the slanting yard there is a pond where you can see the reflection of Mont Orford. At $23,000 it is a bit much, but the view and the land are worth it. We buy it and console ourselves about losing the condo at Club Memphre. Yvon and Roger and Ginette's parents come to visit often. My mother comes once, but she bitches because the fireplace wasn't lit when she got up. She could have gotten it going herself, but she says that she didn't know how … she could burn down a chicken coop for heaven's sake! We fight over this, then we take her back home to Montreal, and we avoid each other for two years afterward.

There are two big stray dogs roaming around: Ti-Lou, a German Shepherd and Jeff, a collie. They belong to no one, but a neighbour feeds them. Ginette has a weakness for dogs. When we are there, she feeds and cuddles them. She brings them inside without worrying about the fleas they will leave behind. The dogs are adorable, but my asthma keeps getting worse. When Yvon and Roger come down we always have a good time building a fire inside the tub of an old washer and roasting wieners at the end of a stick. At times, we go to St. Marguerite where Yvon's parents live. They are very hospitable and have us spend the night at their house.

Now that we have a place in the country, we sell the house on Boisclair. We buy a cheap condo on St. Andre Street next to a very special gay club, where the left side is for the girls, the right for the boys, and the middle for the straights. There's a large stage for dancing and shows. On weekends it gets loud when the club closes at 3 a.m. and everyone is out on the street singing, laughing, and sometimes fighting. It is a good time for us to go down to our cottage!

We are on North Road when we see flames and hear the sirens of the fire brigade. It is our cottage that is burning … the firefighters do not arrive on time to save it. Ginette, the dogs, and I watch the complete destruction of our cottage. Ti-Lou has his head on my foot; he senses that I am sad. The next day, all that is left are a few darkened coins from our card playing. Romeo is very sorry; it was he who lit a fire in the fireplace, not knowing that the metal sheet behind had holes in it. He wanted the cottage to be cozy when we arrived, and no one knew that the fireplace was in that state. It was a hidden issue, and we will be reimbursed by our insurance. We go to Romeo's and have a few good drinks before we lie down to sleep on foam slabs on the floor. I sleep near the patio door, keeping it ajar a little so I can breathe. There are big smokers here.

We have two choices: do nothing or rebuild within the same dimension, 24' x 35'. We visit the prefabs at Maison Bonneville. We arrange for a small two-bedroom house to be delivered. The young man taking the order asks us how we can come in here and place an order without a husband. This would be hard to hear from a much older man but from a young man it is utterly surprising! This is October 1988, after all...

In the meantime, we must have the cement foundation ready, and the septic tank installed. The house arrives the following spring, the two halves on two different trucks. Rails are put down across the foundation, and the two halves are slid along them slowly one after the other. They are joined at the rooftop, and the house is complete. All the neighbours have gathered to watch this procedure. There is still so much to be done! The plumber must solder the pipes and install the extra piping necessary for the wastewater to go to the septic tank. Joints must be pulled before painting and flooring can be put down. We choose to have ceramic tiles throughout because of the dirt we bring in from the unpaved road and what all. At the far end of the living room, we have installed a nice wood-burning fireplace. It is an open area, so that when you enter you see immediately the kitchen, the dining area, and the living room. As we still have the same white dining room set, we paint the walls midnight blue. It is quite stunning for a wee house. I just have enough space left to buy a white pre-owned upright piano. We do all this, Ginette and I, without debts and without a husband. The neighbour across the pond is green with envy.

I ask my employer for a transfer to their Sherbrooke branch, as I am moving to Austin. I get a cashier position which I am completely unfit for. That and the traveling from Montreal to Magog stresses me so much, I cannot breathe. My asthma is so bad that Ginette takes me three times to the emergency of La Providence, Magog's hospital. The third time, they keep me in for a week.

My cousin Richard, youngest son of my Aunt Leola, lives with his partner Serge. He has a good friend Pierre who owns a printing company in Sherbrooke. They need an accountant, and Ginette is hired. At the end of December 1988, we move to Austin while Jacqueline looks for a buyer for our condo in Montreal. I resign from my job, and I am unemployed for a while. I have some spare time, so I go with Romeo to an organic greenhouse where I pick cucumbers and tomatoes from climbing vines. I sort the tomatoes by size, wash them, and put them in small baskets ready for sale. It is mainly from curiosity that I am there. Eventually, I get hired at Pierre's as a receptionist. Beggars can't be choosers!

Almost every second Friday night, Ginette's parents come spend the weekend. They buy their own twin beds for the spare room and a pedal boat. Jean-Paul stacks on the roof of his car all the necessary items to build us a shed. That will keep him busy a good part of the summer, while I play cards with Marguerite or go around the pond in the pedal boat. I pedal and Marguerite pretends to. I make three meals a day while they are here and—although I like them very much—I am glad to see them go on Monday morning!

We now have a very large terrace facing the pond which communicates with the front porch. At the point where the two meet we have a nice wooden screened gazebo. It is lovely to sit there with friends in the evenings, away from the mosquitoes. There are around twenty stray cats hiding under the terrace. We buy big bags of cat food for them and in winter we have a basin with an electric burner in it to keep the water from freezing. There are raccoons that come and eat out of our hands and one skunk. We have so many birds that we no longer put grains in birdfeeders, we scatter the seeds on the terrace instead. We get grosbeaks, blackcap chickadees, juncos, finches, and sparrows. These are the small pleasures of country life.

But I guess this is getting too monotonous for Ginette, and she is ripe for some change. She becomes infatuated with a girl that is a cashier at the bank where she makes the daily deposits. This affair will last three months, and I am heartbroken. I see her struggle with the choice she must make stay with me or move on with her new lover. The girl likes sports and has a dog; I prefer painting and I am allergic to dogs. She is young, and I am fifty-two. I cannot blame her. We put the house up for sale. I am ready to go back to Montreal.

In Montreal, I find out that my mother has developed colon cancer. I am quite sick myself; I must get my gallbladder removed, and I spend ten days in the hospital because of a complication. After recuperating, I spend a few days at Aunt Olida's, and I visit my mother. One afternoon, I decide to go see some of my colleagues from the bank. I get off the elevator on the wrong floor, and I come face-to-face with Marie-Claude, Gaston Cantin's assistant. They need someone to work in the vault to prepare the wills for digitization. It will take three months. I apply for the post and return home … and Ginette has not gone anywhere. After a few days I get a call from Gaston; he recognizes me, and I am hired. I stay at my aunt's during the week and go back home for the weekends. I visit my mother regularly.

After three months, Gaston's assistant goes on maternity leave, and I stay on for a while longer. Gaston is my boss but also a friend. Over lunch we talk about our heartbreaks. His boyfriend Claude has just left him, although they remain good friends. Meanwhile, in Austin, it is hard to find a buyer for the house. Ginette has gone to work for Metro-litho a branch of Transcontinental; she will ask for a transfer to their Montreal office later. My mother is hospitalized. I visit her every day after work. She will never recuperate from that terrible cancer.

Ginette gets her transfer, and we rent an apartment on Cherrier Street. It's good to be living in Montreal again. We help my mother with her groceries and do a little housework for her. She is back in the hospital, and the doctor tells me to find a place for her in a care home. We move her to Magog, where her sister Leola finds her a place close to the hospital. Monic, Andrew, and Lynda also live in Magog, so my mother gets plenty of visitors. We must empty her apartment. She has a lot of worthless things. One thing of value she owns is a beautiful mahogany grandfather clock. Claude's parents buy it and name it Lea.

My mother dies on the 1st of December 1994. While she is still conscious, she tells me, "You did everything you could." Shane comes to the funeral and decides to move back to Montreal. We do not see each other much. We exchange birthday cards and Christmas cards. I think he is ashamed of me.

III

The house in Austin is sold finally, and we buy a condo on Richmond Street. Gaston lives five minutes away from us in a spacious condo befitting his profession. He has many paintings on the walls from well-known artists and a great wood-burning fireplace in his living room. His home reflects his personality, warm and welcoming. We are so proud of having him as a good friend. We are invited to a New Year's Eve party at Guy Sinnette's, a friend of Gaston's, who also works with us. We get to meet Claude, Gaston's ex and forever friend. We have a great time. It is surprising how many gays work quietly in the estate department! Gaston owns a house in Stoneham, outside of Quebec City; we spend a weekend there before he sells it. He then invests in a condo in Bromont where we are invited as well. He likes to have a place to near ski slopes. In winter, he skis a lot on weekends.

Ginette and I decide that we are due for a trip overseas. We decide on Scotland. Sylvie, a friend from the days working at the law firm, now works for a Canadian airline—she gives us two standby passes, and we get to fly for free. We stay a few days in London before taking a bus to Edinburgh. When we get off the bus, we ask a lady where we can find some accommodations. She hooks her arms under ours, leads us to the next corner, and tells us to go down a block and, turn left, where all the bed and breakfasts are located. Such a nice person.

We stay a week at the Acorn, it is walking distance from Prince Street. The stores are filled with souvenirs bearing all manner of tartans. We visit the old castle and a Scotch distillery. We walk the Royal Mile up to Holyrood Palace. While in Scotland, we take a boat ride on Loch Lomond and on Loch Katrine. We visit Stirling Castle and the old cemetery next to it.

Upon returning, Ginette calls her mother. She has bad news: her sister is on life support at the hospital. She has suffered an embolism. She dies at the young age of fifty, leaving three children behind. Ginette is devastated; her sister had been so happy to spend a summer month at a cottage next to us while we still owned the house in Austin. Gaston is the youngest of fourteen; he took care of his dying mother and understands Ginette's sorrow.

The neighbourhood where we live is too noisy; when we visit Yvon and Roger at their house in St. Lambert we get the urge to move again. The condo is put up for sale and is quickly sold by Sid Alavi. Coincidentally, Mr. Alavi knows of a house for sale next to the cemetery in St. Lambert. The lady who owned it had died in her rocking chair, and her son, who lives in Ottawa, is eager to sell. Not everyone wants to buy a house where somebody just died *and* next to a cemetery. We buy the house for the ridiculous price of $144,000. There is work to be done, of course.

We move mid-November 1999. On the day we get in, Gaston comes over with his architect friend, John Semple; they bring a chicken pot pie from Costco. John draws us a quick plan for the kitchen. We hire a contractor who follows the plan to a T. It turns out beautifully. However, we would like a dining room adjoining the living room. We have Robert, Ginette's brother, open the wall between the master bedroom and the living room. We use the smaller room for our bedroom. The bathroom must be renovated as well. While this is being done, we take an organized trip around Italy.

There is still the basement to be redone, but it is summer, and Ginette dreams of owning a swimming pool. We have the space required by the city to have one dug up. We get a nice kidney-shaped pool, surrounded by decorative shrubs and flower beds. There are a few centuries-old maple trees in the yard, and squirrels are running all over the place. Robert builds us a large sun deck; it is all very nice. He brings over his girlfriend Paulette, a sexy blonde. She is very bright and easy to be around. She is uncomfortable next to a cemetery, but once in the pool she forgets about it. We also have a full view of the fireworks given by the city of Montreal every second Saturday in summertime.

On June 1, 2001, I retire from the bank for good. We meet with Murielle, a travel agent in Saint-Lambert. With free passes from Sylvie, we make, yearly, a trip to Europe. We get a pass for Gaston as well and fly to Germany. We arrive first at Frankfurt airport; from there we take a train to Cologne. The first sight we see is the Cathedral—what beauty! We rent a room with a queen-sized bed and a cot; Gaston does not seem to mind sleeping on the cot. We go down the Rhine to Bonn where we visit Beethoven's home. There, displayed on an old piano, are the hearing horns and ear trumpets he used as hearing aids because of his deafness.

We then take a train to Berlin. Once off the train, we search for a room on a display board, there is a lady with her husband standing next to us; she speaks German and offers to help us. She calls a hotel nearby and says that we are five and can we get a room at a fair price. The three of us get a large room with two queen-sized beds and a sofa in between. We cannot believe our luck, and we share a glass of Scotch before retiring. Berlin is a special place, with its west and east sides divided by the remains of a great wall. We visit the Pergamon Museum and the Dom (Berlin Cathedral) on the east side and a high-end department store on the west side. There are also the remains of the cobalt glass interior of Kaiser Wilhelm's Memorial Church that is a must to visit.

From Berlin, we go south to Füssen to visit King Ludwig's Neuschwanstein Castle. We stay at Maison Elizabeth guest house; the owner barely speaks English but serves a nice breakfast of warm rolls and honey—there are bees buzzing around her, but she does not seem to mind! There is a beautiful lake in Füssen with many white and black swans. We return to Berlin by bus on the Romantic Road route. Back in Berlin, we take the train to Prague. We are too late for a train compartment; we must sit on low stools next to the window. There is no restaurant, either. So, we are hungry and uncomfortable while across the aisle there are groups of Germans singing, laughing, drinking, and eating their sausages from a great steaming pot.

When we arrive in Prague, there is a line-up of folks trying to entice us to rent at their place. A young lady hears us speak French; she speaks French as well, and she knows a lady who owns a condominium downtown. She rents the large bedroom and the living room and keeps a room and one of the two bathrooms for herself—we must share the kitchen. At $100 per night, it is a great deal, and we take it. It is right next to the great square with its famous rotating World Clock and to Charles Bridge. There are many churches where one can catch a concert every night. While we are there, we visit the Jewish cemetery and the oldest synagogue of Europe. Ginette and I also visit the Terezin Nazi camp. Gaston is too sensitive to come with us.

Back home, we are a bit discouraged; there is yet so much to do and there is leakage next to the fireplace chimney—we can see a few bubbles forming on the ceiling. We hear of a new development in Brossard, next to the St. Lawrence River; it is a fifty-plus community. It is worth a visit, and we like the model house. It is in an enclosed area with townhouses of assorted colours, depending on the street. The living rooms have cathedral ceilings, some have a mezzanine, and there is a large private patio at the back. All have a private garage. While in the clubhouse we can see the cargo ships go by, and we swim in the pool overlooking the river.

We call June McGarr, a renowned real estate agent in St. Lambert. She sells the house within five days, and we move to our townhouse in the spring of 2003. I make two friends there, both retired. They often come and sit with me on my front balcony. Between the two of them, I know everything that goes on in the village—inwardly, I call one The Gazette and the other La Presse. While living there, I join a small group of people for a Spanish class given by a neighbour. We have a fun time.

John Semple, Gaston's friend, lives in Provincetown, Massachusetts where he owns a two-story house. He did the renovation himself and got some help from Gaston when he went down there in summer. John's friends, Tom and Rex, have a big cottage close to him. They rent it from spring to fall. One fall weekend, we go down with Gaston to visit John. Tom's cottage is empty, and he lets us use it for free while we are there. We leave $200 on the table when we leave, but he mails it back to us, minus twenty-five dollars for utilities. In fact, this is to make us feel better. The following year, we drive down there followed by Gaston and François, one of Gaston's many friends. They come all the way from Montreal on their motorcycles.

Attached to Tom's cottage there is another big house they call "the barn." We stay in the cottage while Gaston and François occupy the barn. We get together for supper, which I and François prepare. We eat around the large table under a ring of wax candles. We make several more friends while we are there. I particularly like Richard, an artist; he is most friendly and enjoys drinking Scotch, as I do. He has a remarkable white moustache and rosy cheeks. Provincetown is a beautiful place to live.

In 2005, bad luck befalls Ginette: she has breast cancer. Before she starts chemotherapy, we go shopping for a wig. As soon as the treatment starts, her hair begins falling out. I shave her head completely; she has a nicely shaped skull. She wears the wig to work so as not to make her co-workers uncomfortable. She never stops working unless she must go for treatments. She is so brave. She does beat it, and when she is feeling good again, we buy a new 2005 indigo blue Toyota Matrix to celebrate. We decide to travel again and opt for Greece where we visit Athens, Santorini, Paros, Crete, Rhodes, and Mykonos. Each island has its own charm.

It is very tiring for Ginette to travel every day for work (from the south shore to Ville StLaurent in the northern part of Montreal) so by 2006 we decide to move back to town. Our next-door neighbour is a real estate agent; it takes him a while to sell our house, but by May 2007 we are back in Montreal. We buy a two-bedroom condominium on De la Montagne Street. The smaller room has been opened into the living room and is used as a dining room, which suits us fine. Sadly, a few weeks before our move, Ginette's dad goes to the hospital to have an artery unblocked and dies there after a few days. He will never see our nice new home.

Now, we are living near Gaston again. He waves at me when he passes by on his way to work. I continue my Spanish classes at the YWCA, just a few blocks up the street. It is great to live downtown again! A friend of Gaston's has just returned from Argentina; he says it's the place to go, the economy there has just hit rock bottom and our Canadian dollars go a long way. We start by visiting Buenos Aires; they call this city South America's Paris. We have a private guide and chauffeur to show us around town for a few dollars.

We book a bus excursion to Ushuaia, the capital of Tierra del Fuego. On our way down we stop at the Perito Morino glacier, one of the most spectacular sights in Patagonia. Further south, at the Valdés Peninsula, we watch the community of elephant seals and sea lions; further down in Punta Tombo we can walk amongst the thousands of Magellan penguins. We take a plane from Punta Tombo to Ushuaia, referred to as "the end of the world;" it is 3,000 kilometres south of Buenos Aires. The native guide takes pride in showing us the one vinyl-sided house in the village. He tells us about the beavers imported from Canada for their fur. Unfortunately, the change of diet made them loose their great fur, and the little ones are born with a very ordinary coat. They have propagated so much that now they have become a source of food. We come back through El Calafate where we partake in a *méchoui* (spit-roast) of sweet-tasting lamb. It was a fabulous vacation.

Back home, I develop severe eczema. I see a dermatologist, Dr. Gratton, who tells me that I probably do not like where I am living, and it's causing the eczema. We hire Paul Patterson, a real estate agent. He has a client from abroad that is looking for a downtown condo for his son who will be attending McGill University. It's a quick sale. Mr. Patterson suggests that we look at a few condos he has for sale on Nun's Island. I visit three while Ginette is at work and fall in love with the last one. Ginette goes to see it after work, and she thinks it's great. We need to take out the rugs and have wooden floors put in. After a few coats of paint, it is ready for us to move in. It is a very big condo on the first floor, with a backyard. We live there happily for a few years.

After thirty-six years of living together, Ginette and I exchange vows in front of a notary. Robert and

Paulette sign the register as witnesses. We toast with fine champagne and share dinner at a good steakhouse on the island. It is Friday the thirteenth, of April 2012.

Yvon and Roger had parted ways a few years before, and Yvon has met Martin—a good-looking man, twenty years younger than himself. They too will marry in April 2012. They live in Saint-Bruno, in a condo owned by Martin. He is super intelligent; no problem is too big for him to solve! I am old enough to be his grandmother, but we get along surprisingly well.

Gaston tours the countryside with a group of motorcyclists. They happen to go through a small village in Lanaudiere, called Lanoraie. The village is directly on the St. Lawrence River. He spots a house for sale next to the dock and asks to go in and look around. He discusses the price with the vendor and makes an offer to purchase. He buys the house but cannot occupy it for six months. Meanwhile, he sells his condo in Bromont. As soon as he can move in, he invites us to come and visit. We spend many afternoons there with him. On a special occasion, we are invited to go for a celebration supper and stay over. We are quite a few friends there, singing out loud and having a great time! The next-door neighbour, Chéryl, and her girlfriend Nadia comment on our fine voices the following morning. What a fine place to live!

Ginette is sixty-one years old. We make a great effort to pay off the mortgage so that she can retire soon. We put the condo up for sale while Gaston looks around Lanoraie for a house we might like. We visit many; it takes time. With his help we finally visit one that could suit us. It is directly on the river and has been modernized recently. It is a good solid house. We meet the owners; they live a little way down the road. They are asking $285,000. The price is good, but we have not sold our condo on Nun's Island, yet. Luckily, we do get a decent offer soon afterwards. We call back Denis Desrochers, the owner of the house we have decided to buy. The price as gone up to $319,00, since a lady had made such an offer—however, she opted out of the deal. We remind him that he told us the price was $285,000. He is a very decent fellow, and he says okay. We meet with him and Jocelyne, his wife, the following Saturday. We present our offer scribbled on a piece of paper, which he accepts. He even lets us move in a few weeks before going to the notary. The house needs a few additions. We have a wood-burning fireplace and an air-conditioner installed as soon as we move in. We start inviting our friends over. We are so proud of ourselves.

We can now walk to Gaston's house. Every time we go say hello, we speak with the girls next door. They are both charming in their own ways. Chéryl is a businesswoman, she has a cleaning company. She has owned her house for twenty years and knows everything that goes on in the neighbourhood. Nadia was born in Africa to Lebanese parents. She speaks a beautiful French. They are both bilingual. We develop, slowly but surely, a strong friendship with them.

Ginette has two more weeks to go before retiring. The company organizes a great good-bye party for her. She is greatly appreciated by her superior and loved by her colleagues. Then, we take a trip to Turkey. We particularly enjoy Istanbul with its mosques, the markets, and the many cats. We take a nice boat ride on the Bosphorus Strait.

When we return home, as an addition to the veranda, we have a very large sundeck built at the back so that we can sit with a coffee in the morning and watch the sun come up. We can see the cruise ships coming from afar. So many get together with friends and relatives in that house! At times, Yvon and Martin come for supper and a sleepover. When they go on vacations, they bring us their cats to mind for a few weeks.

Ginette's mother now lives in an old folk's home; Ginette visits her every Saturday afternoon. On Sundays we go with Chéryl and Nadia to see movies in English on the south shore. There are no movies presented in

English where we live; I find that particularly irksome. I soon realize that a house is a lot of work ... all that lawn mowing in summer and snow shovelling in winter gets to us after a while.

For a little bit of excitement, Gaston, Ginette, and I decide to take horseback-riding lessons. At seventy-four, I get on a big black stallion and learn how to trot. The teacher doesn't want me to canter in case I fall and break something. Every September, around Ginette's birthday, we still go down to Ogunquit. We introduce Chéryl and Nadia to the place, and they just love it. Nadia can't get enough of the lobster rolls.

Monic, Andrew, and Lynda have moved to Victoria, BC. They keep sending us literature on James Bay, the neighbourhood where they live. We might join them someday, but for now we cannot go too far from Ginette's mother. However, we put the house up for sale—in this unknown town, it takes years to sell a house.

Margaret dies at the ripe old age of ninety-four. We are free to live anywhere. Strangely enough, on my birthday, January 19, 2019, we get an offer to purchase greater than we had hoped for. We put Lynda and Monic in charge of finding us a nice apartment in the building next to theirs. We sign our lease without even having seen the apartment, call the movers, and on the twentieth of April we take the Trans-Canada Highway in our brand-new Honda Civic filled to the brim, and head for Victoria.

How beautiful and breathtaking this city is! Monic and Lynda are waiting for us; they have the key to our apartment. Upon opening the door, we have a full view of the Pacific. I think I am dreaming. It surpasses our expectations.

We must wait for our furniture to arrive. Meanwhile, we have two folding garden chairs, an air mattress, and all the dishes and small appliances that we need.

There are so many great things around to discover. First, we can get to the water in ten minutes and walk along the never-ending path. There are plenty of benches along the way if you need to rest. There's the breakwater that is so long it takes twenty minutes to get to the end of it. Ten minutes away, there's Beacon Hill Park with its many ponds full of ducks and geese and turtles. Flowers and bushes are attended to daily by gardeners and to top it all, there's a petting zoo filled mainly with little goats that you are allowed to pet and brush. Peacocks are everywhere, screeching and showing off. There's the harbour with its yachts, sailboats, and water taxis. Many huge cruise ships land here all summer, and the tourists take rides on the many horse-drawn carioles. Across the street, there's a supermarket, a drugstore, a liquor store, two pubs, and a Chinese restaurant. What more can you ask for?

Our building was built in 1958, and we receive our mail through a slot in the door. It is a very comfortable apartment, in an old-fashioned sort of way. There are no screens; they are not necessary because there's no mosquitoes here, and best of all there's no winter. People in Victoria are very courteous and greet you when they pass by you on your morning walk, but they keep to themselves.

However, after a few months we start missing our good times with our friends. We miss them so much that when September comes, we take a plane to Montreal to visit for a few days. They are very happy to see us; they spoil us which makes it worse for us when we return.

After less than a year, we decide to return to Quebec at the end of our lease. We ask our friends Gaston, Cheryl, and Nadia to look around for somewhere nice for us to live, not too far from where they live. In Repentigny there's a new development by the St. Lawrence River. It seems perfect for us. We sign the lease for occupation the first of May 2020.

Meanwhile, we go to Vietnam to celebrate my eightieth birthday. We stay in nice little unit with a backyard next to a river. At night, we watch the fishermen come back along the river with lit lanterns on their boats. It is very nice to watch. In the daytime there are plenty of white egrets flying around. We take several excursions; we even ride in a rickshaw in full traffic. We visit a temple filled with people moving incense sticks in prayer. It smells great, but the air is so thick you can hardly breathe.

Upon our return, we get ready for our move back. There is the COVID-19 pandemic that will make the six days on the road very difficult. Very few hotels and restaurants are open.

The apartment is very modern, quite a change from where we have come from. COVID makes it impossible to visit our friends. Folks my age are asked to stay inside; we are blamed for spreading the disease. The Prime Minister is overzealous; he imposes a curfew: no leaving the house after 8 p.m. unless you must walk the dog. Police officers check license plates to make sure people are not visitors but residents. Everybody lives through two years of hell. We also get the sad news that Andrew has died at the end of March 2021.

We decide later to fly over to Victoria for a few weeks. I take a walk on the path by the water as I did before. I stop at a bench where I read on the plaque, "Today, I found paradise." Suddenly, I know that here, in Victoria, is where I belong. I return to Monic's; Lynda and Ginette are there. I tell them that I want to move back. Ginette is overjoyed. We go meet the administrator; she will have an apartment available next spring. We must honour our lease anyway. It works fine. We spend eighty-five days in Torremolinos, Spain, during the winter, and when we return, we hit the road again for Victoria. We are in our apartment by May 1, 2023. The view is stupendous; the apartment is old but cheerful. We could stay here for a long time.

Perhaps this nomad has put down her bindle for good…

About the Author

I came back from school at 9 years old to find our modest belongings by the side of the road. The bailiff had changed the padlock, so I sat there alone and humiliated for a while, waiting for my mother to come home. It was the moment in my life that made me who I am: a nomad.

www.ingramcontent.com/pod-product-compliance
Lightning Source LLC
LaVergne TN
LVHW011729060526
838200LV00051B/3091